I Love My 'Puter

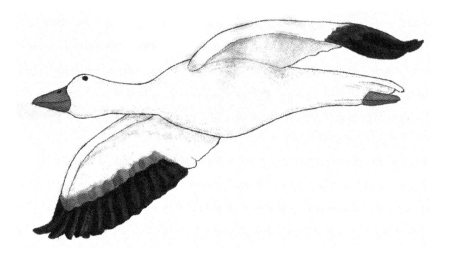

Illustration of Snow Goose sculpture by Cindy Robison
Snow Goose sculpture by Martha Shade

Come Fly Away With Me

Come fly away with me
and have some fun.
You'll be so much happier
when we're done.

If computers have confused
and puzzled you before,
take this book to your computer
and fear no more.

Computers can be Fun!
And pleasing to look at, too.
With this book learn valuable skills,
and create fun projects that are new.

When you have finished
my little book,
open the doors of your imagination
and take a look.

Then loosen those chains,
that so often surround the creative parts,
and let yourself Soar
while you listen to your Heart.

Blessings to you all…
Cindy Robison

I Love My 'Puter

A fun computer book for beginners!

Cindy Robison

Authors Choice Press
San Jose New York Lincoln Shanghai

I Love My 'Puter
A fun computer book for beginners!

Authors Choice Press
an imprint of iUniverse.com, Inc.

For information address:
iUniverse.com, Inc.
5220 S 16th, Ste. 200
Lincoln, NE 68512
www.iuniverse.com

ISBN: 0-595-14265-6

Printed in the United States of America

To computer beginners everywhere…
May your 'puter path be filled with sunshine and joy!

Table of Contents

Introduction and Acknowledgments

With any creative endeavor that any of us are committed to at any given time in our lives, there are moments when that negative voice creeps in and says things like, "What...are you doing? Why are you doing this? This is stupid and a waste of time!" I've had those moments while writing this book. What kept me going with this idea was the knowledge that there were probably many people who learned the way I do, by taking one simple step at a time. I also knew that many people were closet artists like me. Your heart and soul yearns to create beautiful things and yet you feel stifled and unsure. I love to paint, write, and sew. There is a wonderful fullness that I feel inside of me when I can and do create. It brings me joy and peace. I've found that I have these same feelings when I am creating with my computer; whether it be a special card, an email for a friend, or a story about something that is important to me. I wanted this book to be a source, not only, of practical and simple knowledge about the computer for beginners, but also a source of encouragement for those who love to be creative.

There are many people in my life that have been and are now sources of encouragement for me. They are dear friends who tell me, when I have listened too closely to that negative voice, that I must listen to my heart. They help me to remember, when I get into those small tight places, that life is very short and that to live fully and with grace I have be who I am and express myself creatively in whatever way that may be. So, my gratitude and love goes out to the people who have encouraged and supported me during the creation of this book; Mari, Martha,

Sandi, Jan, Kerrie, Sharon, Milli, Barbara, and Laurel. And to all of the people who are now in my life or who have come and gone in my life and have inspired and encouraged me, I thank you all as teachers and guides. I hope that I have given back to all of you, what you have so lovingly given to me.

When I first got my computer, there were people in my life at the time who were encouraging me to write. So, I began dabbling in writing as a creative outlet again. I rediscovered my love of writing when working on my computer. It is such an enjoyable machine for me to write on. I can delete, cut and paste to move around text, add to, change, etc., and do all of these menial tasks, that used to drive me nuts with a regular typewriter, with incredible ease. But, I had no focus and no idea where this new writing path would lead me. I decided not to worry about it and began to just enjoy the experience of writing again. During this time, I had a bizarre, touching, and oddly beautiful experience with a flock of honking snow geese flying in a V formation near my home. Yes…I did say snow geese. You're probably wondering what I'm talking about, right? Well, I won't go into a lot of detail about the experience except to say that it was surreal and at first startling. It was one of those experiences that makes you stop and shake your head and wonder, 'Did that just really happen?'

I shared my experience with two of my trusted friends, Mari and Martha. They were excited. One thing led to another and the next thing I knew, another friend, Sandi had sent me a passage about the snow goose from a book titled *Animal-Speak* by Ted Andrews, i.e. *The Call of the Quest, The Keynote for the Goose*. She felt that it would help me to gain some understanding of the significance of my unusual goose experience. This is a book filled with stories about different animals and their sacred meanings. It tells you how to identify your animal totem. It also tells you about animals that make a sudden appearance in your life and what that animal's appearance means. Well, the snow goose wasn't my totem, but I had just had a pretty weird experience with a flock of them. My friends assured me that the experience was significant and related to my present circumstances. So, I read the passage from Ted Andrews' book…and it gave me goose bumps.

Apparently, the snow goose, which is white with black wing tips, is a totem that can help you with written communication. The excerpt from the book went into the symbolism behind different aspects of the snow goose like it's honking call, how and why flocks of geese fly in a V formation, and the migration habits of geese. What was so interesting was that it all seemed to pertain directly to what was happening in my life at that moment. I realized that my unusual experience was one of those coincidental happenings that make you really sit up and think.

After reading this passage, I decided that I was indeed meant to begin writing again. After hearing my goose story, my friend Martha Shade, who is an amazing sculptor here in Taos, NM, told me that she wanted to create a snow goose sculpture for me (see illustration at the beginning of the book.) It has been such a special heart gift. The sculpture has a very feminine presence and I have affectionately named her Felicia. She hangs suspended from the ceiling above my computer looking as though she is forever in majestic flight. My snow goose symbolizes to me the fact that writing is a very important creative outlet for me. Martha and Sandi also gave me, simultaneously without either of them knowing it at the time, a lovely poem by Mary Oliver titled *Wild Geese* from her book *Dream Work* that again seemed to speak directly to my life at the time.

Well, I began having dreamy visions of myself sitting at my computer composing the great American novel. In this vision, words flowed magically from my fingertips as I typed on my new computer. During this time, friends began asking me for help with their computers. I started writing down simple instructions for them. I found that I really enjoyed typing out these instructions. I loved helping people, who were beginners like me, with their computers. I woke up one morning and thought, 'I'm going to write a book for beginners!' and *I Love My 'Puter* was born. Words did begin to flow from my fingertips as I typed on my new computer, but my visions of a great novel were gone, for the time being anyway. Instead, I tapped into this amazing surge of energy to write a book that I hoped would help people enjoy their computers as much as I enjoyed mine. I know that the encouragement and support that I received, while I was creating my little book, helped to bring it to fruition and I am so grateful to you all.

When I first began learning on my computer, there were two books that I used for general reference before I started experimenting and playing on my own. One was the Microsoft Word 97/ Microsoft Works book titled *Getting Results with Microsoft Word 97* that came with my computer. My kudos go out to the group of people who obviously worked very hard to develop MS Word. To put it simply, I love this program. If you haven't visited their website yet, it's a good place to visit occasionally to find out about new updates. Their website address is microsoft.com. The other book was called *Computer Friendly* by Raymond Steinbacher and published by Green Tree Press, Inc. This book is geared more towards the simple technical things you need to know when getting started with your first computer. It was very easy to understand and well written. You can find out more about this book and others like it by visiting the Green Tree Press, Inc. website at green-treepress.com.

I'd also like to extend a special Thank You to everyone at iUniverse. The publishing program that you have set up for print on demand publishing is truly a great one. If you're an author and would like to know more about their publishing program, you can visit their website at iUniverse.com.

And now onto the book itself, I hope that you enjoy your journey.

1

My 'Puter Story

I love my computer and I want to help you to love yours. Even now, I'm smiling as I write this statement, because I never imagined that I would love a computer. If someone had told me one year ago that very soon I would buy my first computer, set it up, learn how to operate it, teach myself how to be creative with it, and have fun with it, I would have laughed and said, "No Way!"

I bought my first computer at the age of 41. I decided that I needed to 'get with it.' The problem was, I was terrified of computers. My first computer experience happened years ago, when I took several computer classes. The classroom that I taught in had a computer for the students to use and I needed to learn more about it. Even after two courses, I still didn't understand how to use it. This was back when you had to type in keyboard prompts and there was no such thing as a mouse. Whenever I went to try something on it, I would have to ask Jason, one of my students, for help. "Jason," I would ask, "how do I turn this thing on?" He would look at me, roll his eyes, giggle into his hand, and reply, "Ohhhhhh, Cindy." Then he would proceed to turn the computer on and whiz away into computerland. I would stand behind him thinking that I was never going to understand. And for whatever reason, be it a mental block or just fear, I never was able to understand. After that, I just gave up. I did work again once on a computer, occasionally, doing simple things like entering names, addresses, and inputting information into a form letter; but I had no clue as to how to do more than that.

Fifteen years later, I was sitting at my desk at work looking at that machine again. Using a computer was something I needed to do on a limited basis for my job. Everyone now had a mouse. You no longer had to type in shortcuts, unless you wanted to. Navigation with the mouse was supposed to be easy. I was told that anyone could learn to use computers and that it would be a snap for me to learn now. I felt somewhat hopeful. The terror was still there.

Before I started the job, I had taken a few private lessons from a computer consultant to learn more about the advances that had been made. At $35 an hour I could only justify taking a few. The man who tried to teach me was a very patient, kind, and intelligent man. However, I feared he would raise his hands to his head at any moment, grab handfuls of his hair and scream, "You bloody idiot!" He didn't, but I worried that he wanted to. I was so afraid that I would do something wrong that just moving the mouse without jerking became a lesson in focus and relaxation. I couldn't seem to learn. I told him it was a good starting place for me when we were done. Leaving his home, I felt despair. I still didn't get it.

I got by with just doing simple things on my computer at my job. I took time to work through the tutorial that came with the computer. When I left the job, I felt somewhat relieved that I wouldn't have to look at that computer anymore sitting on my desk. But a seed of curiosity had been planted. It did seem a little easier. And now, I knew how to turn it on and get into the word processing program. I had also observed several people doing simple graphics with their computers. Seeing this definitely caught my attention. I considered the possibility of learning more and tentatively planned on going to the local library to try and learn more on the computers that they had available for the public.

A friend had been coaxing me to buy one for a long time. She had gotten a great deal on one. "Why don't you just call and find out more?" she asked. So, I called and asked for more information. When I got the computer catalog, I went numb. That cold prickly feeling started in my stomach and spread quickly throughout my body. Nothing on any of the pages of the catalog made any sense to me. The next time we talked she asked me again, "When are you going to get a computer?" "Well," I said, "I think I'm going to wait. Besides, I really don't have the room. Where would I put it?" I have a very small apartment and the only place that I had any room was one small corner of my bedroom. When I made my excuses and she seemed to accept that I just wasn't ready, I felt relieved. But, she didn't stop asking. My curiosity grew.

One day my curiosity grew larger than my fear. I decided that I could at least call Gateway computers and ask to speak to a sales rep. I could explain my lack of knowledge and ask for help. The space problem in my apartment could be examined. Cost and accessories could be discussed and hopefully thoroughly and simply explained; twice if need be. I picked up the phone and dialed.

My conversation with the young man was progressing pleasantly and easily. He understood that it was my first computer and that I knew virtually nothing. His reassuring attitude helped me to realize that many people, who are buying their first computers, felt the same fear that I was experiencing. Patiently and slowly he answered all of my questions. I began to feel at ease and knew that I would get off the phone with not only my dignity intact, but also some more knowledge under my belt. I would be able to make a more informed decision when I was ready to buy.

However, I still had to figure out my space problem. Then he asked, "Cindy, are you ready to order your first computer?" I replied, "Well, no. I still haven't figured out where I will put it. The only place I have to put it is in a small corner of my bedroom. I have a card table to set it up on, but that isn't going to be enough room for all of the stuff that comes with the monitor." "You're in luck!" he said. A new model had just come out called the Astro. The hard drive, floppy disk drive, CD-ROM, and speakers were all encased in the same unit as the monitor. I got out my tape measure. I measured and then measured again. With this new computer, I would even have room for a small printer.

Well, the rest is history as they say. I got off the phone and realized that I had just ordered my first computer. UPS delivered it a week later and I was at once overwhelmed again. A huge box, which looked like a cow, was sitting in the middle of my living room. I wondered if maybe I should hire someone to put it together for me. Then I remembered that the young man had told me it would be very easy to put together, and, of course, instructions were included. I decided that I would at least try and if I couldn't figure it out, then I would call someone. I not only hooked up my computer and the printer; I also entered all of the information from my ISP without a hitch. After surmounting what was for me a huge hurdle, I felt confident that I could finally begin learning.

Soon after I first got my computer, people started asking me if I had different types of software installed on it. I would feel a mild panic. Here they were asking me about software add-ons and I still hadn't even figured out how to do many of the things my computer came with. There was so much to learn and even more to research. I wanted to know how to be creative with my computer. I considered myself an artist and I loved to do creative things. I worried that in order to do fun and creative things; I would need sophisticated software. It was all almost too much.

Finally, I decided I needed to just put all of that out of my mind and concentrate on the basics. The essence of learning anything, I believe, begins with the decision to start. Usually, for me, the hardest thing to do is to take that first step. What I learned as I began and then toddled along (and, yes, I fell down frequently) was that I could do a lot of fun and very creative projects on my computer with the programs that were installed when I got it. I didn't need new software programs to do creative things. Don't get me wrong, new software is great. In fact, I recently purchased a good graphics software program that I know will expand my creative capabilities. The point is, though, that I didn't need it to begin being creative on my computer and neither do you. I plan on learning more as I go along because I like to grow and learn. But, that is for the future. This is now.

I'm not a computer expert, technician, or web designer. Although, lately, I have been calling myself a computer nerd because I spend a lot of time on my computer and I love working on it. I still don't understand a lot of technical terms or how to do a lot of things on my computer. I am a computer infant. A beginner who has taught herself that computers don't have to be scary or intimidating or even difficult. What they can be is fun!

I decided that all of the fun things that I taught myself to do as a beginner would be great content for a book. I wrote the book the way I taught myself, simple step by simple step. I think that this is the way a lot of people learn. Because I am a beginner, I think that I understand and can speak easily to all of you who are beginners. I know from my experiences over the last few months how intimidating it can be to try and learn something without much support. Hopefully, this book will provide you with the support that you need. *I Love My 'Puter* is the book that I wish I had found to use, when I first started out with my new computer.

I now think of my computer as an amazing creative tool. Your computer can also be set up to be very visually appealing. Take a moment and think of your home. You've probably decorated it with furniture, pictures, and items that reflect your decorating preferences and favorite colors. You've personalized it so that when you come home you like what you see and you feel comfortable in your surroundings. You can do the same thing with your computer. You'll see the colors and images you love and feel inspired and ready to create. If you're going to be working on a computer, I believe that you should really enjoy how your computer screen looks and sounds. Working on a computer that has colors and images that make you feel good can only enhance your over-all experience. Looking at a monitor with gray colors all day is not only going to bring you down, it will put you to sleep. You can brighten and color it up!

Even with little or no knowledge you can learn how to have fun with your computer. As beginners we have to start somewhere and I've set up the instructions so that they are very easy to follow. This book is for beginners who have gotten frustrated with computer classes because they were too advanced for them. It is for those of you who have gotten consultations from computer consultants and didn't understand much of what they said. I know, I understand, I was afraid to ask, too, when they talked about something I didn't understand. I didn't want to appear stupid. It's for those of you who don't have the time to try and figure it out for yourself. And finally, it's for those of you who have tried to read computer books, but gave up because they just didn't give sim-ple enough step by step information. When I started, I wanted a fun book that was based on the assumption, when it was being written, that the people who would be reading it were beginners. I was able to find general answers on how to do many things, but I wanted simple detailed instructions on how to do fun, colorful, and creative things, also. Mostly, I learned by trial and error, experimenting, and playing. I taught myself in the privacy of my home where I could make mistakes and not worry what anyone might think.

If you are a beginner, like I was and still am, this book is for you. If you enjoy doing fun things, if you love color and like to make things visually appealing, and if you are technically challenged like me, then this book is definitely for you. And please notice that I did not say that this book is for dummies. Anyone learning something new is not dumb. We are intelligent beginners.

I'm looking forward to learning more as I go along the computer path. However, my motto has become, Take a big breath and keep it simple! I don't need to be a computer techie to thoroughly enjoy the experience of having a computer. There are many, many things that I can do right now with limited knowledge and experience. And…I'm here to show you that you can, too.

In the back of this book, you'll find reference pages for fonts and symbols. You'll find, also, a fun email attachment that I sent to a friend. When I was writing this book, I considered also including examples of the projects that we will be creating together. I thought that it might help you to see an example of the finished product. I finally decided against doing this. In this book, I've given you specific step by step instructions on how to create fun projects. But, I don't want you to feel obligated to create something exactly the way I did. When you've finished a project, if you don't like the way it looks, play around with it. The main reason I wanted to do specific projects was just to help you see the creative options and possibilities available to you. I've often found, too, that some of my most creative ideas have come from making mistakes. Of course, I don't really think of them as mistakes anymore. So, if you think you've made a mistake, take another look. It may be creative genius at work instead.

Please take a moment to glance through the topics covered in the chapters. As you read my book and follow the steps in each chapter, you will be learning valuable skills that will help you with anything you do try to do on your computer. The skills that you will learn in one chapter will help you in the next chapter. So, instead of skipping around, I would suggest that you begin with Chapter 2 and practice and play your way through each one after that.

I wrote this book based on my knowledge of Windows 98 2nd Edition. If you have an older or updated version, I'm sure that you will still be able to use this book to help you. Don't be bound by limitations. Take some time to consider the possibilities, and then take your new *I Love My 'Puter* book to the computer with you and start having fun. And hopefully very soon you'll love your computer, too!

2

Bring Your Desktop Alive With Color

Before we get started, I want you to do something. Think of your favorite colors. Now, find items in your home that have these colors on them. It could be a throw pillow, tablecloth, picture, color chip, shoe, etc. Just an item to keep close at hand that has colors on it that you love, while you are personalizing your desktop. These items are just for visual reference. You'll want to look at them later on when we make the appearance of your computer visually appealing to you by incorporating the colors you love. Now let's get started!

Desktop Wallpaper or Background Picture

When you first turn on your computer, you will arrive at what is known as your Desktop. On the left-hand side you will see icons with writing beneath them. Your taskbar is on the bottom. The background picture is probably a wallpaper picture that was installed with your computer. Usually, the desktop wallpaper that is installed with your computer is one that you would probably like to change. Mine came with a green background and the signature cow symbol box for Gateway computers. It was fine, but I wanted to personalize and customize my desktop. You can, too. With Windows 98 2nd edition, you will have several ways to go about doing this. We are going to experiment first to acquaint you with some of the features before you choose what you want. So settle back and have some fun!

-Click once on the Start button in the lower right-hand corner of your screen and move your pointer up to Settings so that it is highlighted. You don't need to hold the mouse button down to do this. There is a black arrow ▶ next to Settings that will open up the next menu. Slide your pointer over to Control Panel so that it is highlighted and click once. A window will open up for the Control Panel.

-Find and then place your pointer over Display, in the Control Panel list, and double click.

-A new window will open up that says Display Properties at the top. Below that will be tabs that say Background/ Screensaver/ Appearance/ Effects/ Web/ Settings. Find and click once on the Background tab. You will now see a small image of your computer. Below that you will see Wallpaper and then Select an HTML Document or picture. Next, will be a list of different wallpapers you can choose from in the white box. Click once on the first one, which will probably say None. You'll notice that the screen on the small computer image is now a plain color.

-Now, click once on the button to the right that says Patterns. A new window will open up with a list of different patterns to choose from. Click once on each pattern to highlight it. The Preview thumbnail will show you what each one looks like. This is just to give you an idea of your options. You can choose Patterns as your background picture or you can use patterns to border a picture that you have centered on your desktop. Now click the ✖ button in the upper right-hand corner of the Pattern window to close this window.

-Take some time and click once on each of the wallpapers listed in the white box. You'll notice that you will be able to see what each one looks like on the screen of the small image of your computer.

-After you have viewed them all, pick the one that you liked the best and highlight it by clicking once on it. Now, look to the lower right where it says Display. Below this will be a small white box with a down arrow ▾. Click once on the arrow to see the drop down menu.

-Now you'll see Center, Stretch, and Tile. Click once on each title and notice how the desktop picture changes on the small screen. Some of the pictures, if they are HTML documents, won't have this display feature. If the drop down box is faded out you won't be able to change the screen to center, stretch or tile. Which one did you like best? Click on it again so the desktop wallpaper looks just the way you want it. If you chose to Center your picture there are several ways you can change the border. You can either leave it a solid color, which we will work on later, or you can choose one of the Patterns that you viewed earlier.

-This will be your desktop picture for the time being. You can change it later if you want to. Now look down to the bottom right-hand corner and find the button that says Apply and click it once. Tada! This is now your desktop picture. Remember that it's not set in stone and you can change it at any time.

Your Color Scheme

-Now we're going to personalize the appearance of your computer by applying the colors that you love. You can also personalize your computer with colors that will go with the desktop wallpaper that you have chosen. Look up to the top of your Display Properties window and find the tab that says Appearance. Put your pointer over it and click once. You will now see a new setup that has images with these titles at the top, Inactive Window, Active Window, and Message Box. Below that you will see the titles Scheme:, Item:, and Font:. Each of these titles will have a white box below them with a down arrow that will show a drop down menu when you click on it.

-First, I want you to familiarize yourself with the different options for Scheme: that have already been installed on your computer. This is the list of Schemes that you will see when you click on the down arrow below the title Scheme:. Go ahead and click once on the down arrow, then click the up arrow ▲ that will be directly below the down arrow until the scroll bar is at the top of the list. You can also click on the scrollbar, hold the mouse button down, and move your mouse up to move it to the top.

-Now, click once on each of the Schemes to highlight them. You'll notice that the images in the top box change each time to reflect the colors that are chosen for that particular scheme. This list is important because when you set and apply your personalized schemes you will want to save them in this list. Each time you change your desktop screen wallpaper you will be able to go to this window, view the Scheme list, and find the colors that you previously chose to go with that particular desktop picture. We'll learn how to do this later. For now, check out all of the installed Schemes by clicking once on each of them.

-Now, go to the title Item: and click once on the down arrow next to the white box. Another list will appear. Click the up arrow to move the list to the top. The top item should be 3D Objects. Click once on it to highlight it. It should now appear in the white box below Item:. 3D objects are the areas in any window that seem to stand out from the rest. Keep in mind that visually it's usually best to use a lighter shade of any color for the 3D objects. Think about what color you might want to use.

-To the right of this you will see the title Color: with a box below it displaying the current 3D objects color and a down arrow for the drop down menu. Click once on the down arrow to see the drop down menu display, which will be a color chart. At the bottom you will see a button that says Other. Click once on this button.

-A new window will open that is called Color. Below this you will see Basic Colors: with boxes of different colors below it and to the right of this a color spectrum. Try to find the color box under Basic Colors that is close to the color you have decided on for your 3D objects. Don't worry if it isn't exactly the shade you want, because you can adjust it.

When you have found the color box that is close to the color you have in mind, click once on it. Now, look to the right of the color spectrum. You'll see a vertical box with graduated shades of the same color. This box will change when you click on a color to reflect where that particular color fits in that spectrum.

-To the right of this vertical box you will see a left pointing arrow ◀. Put you pointer over it, click your left mouse button if you are right-handed or your right mouse button if you are left-handed and hold it. Now move your pointer up and down. In the color preview box below the color spectrum you'll see the color you chose change as you move the arrow up and down with your pointer. Play with it until you find the shade that you like. When you're done, move your pointer down and then find and click on the button that says Add to Custom Colors. This will add your personal color to the boxes below the title Custom Colors:. Now go to the button in the lower left-hand corner that says OK and click it once.

-You'll now be back in the Display Properties window. You'll see that the 3D borders around the Inactive, Active, and Message Boxes have changed to the color that you chose. What do you think? Do you like it? If not, you can go back and repeat the previous steps to find another shade of the color that you like or to change to another color.

-Below the Color box that you just worked in to set your 3D-object color, you will see another Color: title with a color box and drop down menu. This new color is for the font that you see on the 3D objects. For instance, the set font color for 3D objects right now is the font color that you see on the tab titles Background/ Screensaver/ Appearance/ Effects/ Web/ Settings. What would you like this font color to be? Follow the previous steps to find a color that you'd like to correspond with the 3D object's color that you've chosen.

-When you've found the color that you want, click once on the OK button to go back to the Display Properties window. Then, click once on the button in the lower right-hand corner that says Apply.

-Look up to the top of the window and find where the tabs say Background/ Screensaver/ Appearance/ Effects/ Web/ Settings. Do you like the color of the font? Does it correspond with the color you chose for 3D objects? If not, you can go back and adjust the color by following the previous steps.

-Now, go back to the box below the title Item:. Click once on the down arrow and then click once on the next item below 3D objects titled Active Title Bar. Notice how more titles and boxes light up. You should now be able to see Size:, Color:, Color 2:, and below that Font:, Size:, Color:, B (for Bold font), and / (for Italic font). Lot's of choices! More fun! Let's get to work.

Note: In order for you to put two colors that will blend nicely on your Active Title Bar, you will need to have your computer colors set higher than 256 colors. Gradient is not available if your computer is set to 256 colors. To check this, click the Settings tab at the top right of your Display Properties window. Look for the title Colors and the white box underneath it. What does it say? If it's set at 256 colors you won't be able to access the gradient for the Active Title Bar. I have my computer set at, True Color (24bit). Click the down arrow next to the white box and see what is available. If you see True Color (24bit) on the list, you can highlight it and click once on it to access this feature. This will slow your computer down a little bit, but I think it's worth it because your computer will now show many colors and images will look real. Click again on the Appearance tab once you have done this.

-Next to Active Title Bar you'll see Size:. Below Size: you'll see a box with numbers in it. Next to this you'll see little tiny up and down arrows. (Aren't they cute!) Play around with these arrows by clicking on them. Notice how the Active, Inactive, and Message Box title bars change in size as you go up or down. I like mine set at about size 24. What size do you like? When you've found the size that you like leave it at that number.

-Next, go to the right of the Size: title to the Color: and Color 2: titles and the boxes below them. With these two Color boxes you will be able to beautifully blend two of your favorite colors. These two colors will be displayed on the Active Title Bar and the Message Box Bar. The first title Color: will be the color that you see on the far left of the Active Title Bar. This will blend into the color you pick from the Color 2: list. Think about what two colors you want to use for these areas.

-Click on each of the color box drop down menus to find your colors as you have in previous steps and then click once on them. Adjust shading if you need to and then click the OK button when you've got your colors just right. Watch the Active Title and Message Box Bars change as you choose your colors. Do they go well together and appeal to you? If not, repeat the previous steps until you've found the colors you like.

-Turn to the back of your book and find the Font page to view all of the different fonts available for you to use. Decide on some different fonts that you really like.

-Click on the down arrow next to the white box below Font: and scroll through the list until you've found the fonts that you think will go well with your color scheme. Experiment with the different fonts that you chose to see which one you like best by clicking once on each font so that it appears in the white box. Now, look up at the Inactive Window, Active Window, and Message Box Bars. Do you like the way the font looks? When you've decided on the font that you want to use, leave it in the white box.

-Next, go to the Size: title that is to the right of Font:. Click on the down arrow to view the different sizes that you can make your font. Click on some of them so that you can see how the font will look with the different sizes. Leave it at the size that you like.

-The Color: title and white box below it next to Size: is where you will determine what color you want the font to be. What color corresponds with your two favorite colors on the Active and Message Box bars? If your two favorite colors for the bars are a dark shade, you will need to pick a font color that is light in shade (white, gold, yellow, or a very light shade of any color.) If your colors are light, you'll need to pick a dark font color. Pick your font color.

-Next to Size: you will see two buttons with B and / on them. Click once on the B, this will make the font Bold. If you like your font bold, leave the button clicked in. If you don't want your font to be bold, click the B again to make it regular.

-Next, click the button with the /. This will make your font italic. Check your font. If you like it italic, you can leave the button clicked in. If you don't, click the button again to make your font regular. Note: Some fonts are already italicized and will not change when you click this button.

-Go back to the Item: title and click the down arrow. The next item on the drop down menu will be Active Window Border. Click once on it so that it appears in the white box.

-To the right of this you'll see the Size: title. Click on the tiny up and down arrows to try out the different sizes that you can make your window border. Watch the Inactive, Active, and Message Box Bars as you do this. They will shrink in size with more of a border as you go up in size and visa versa. Find the size that you like and leave it.

-To the right of the Size: title you'll see the Color: title. Find the color that you would like the border to be. You can either pick a corresponding color to the 3D objects color or use the same color as the 3D objects. I usually use a darker shade of the color that I chose for the 3D Objects. If you use a darker shade or corresponding color, it will provide a wonderful framing effect for the window. Find the color you want for your border.

-Click once on the next Item: on the drop down menu titled Application Background. The color you pick for this will not be readily visible when you choose it. You'll see this color in the background of some of the windows that you open and work in. For instance, when you are working on a word document in Microsoft Word, the application background is the area behind the document if you have your Zoom set at 75% or lower (we'll cover Zoom later.) The application color will be the color you choose now. I usually pick a color that is a few shades darker than the color that I chose for the 3D objects.

-Click once on the next Item: on the drop down menu titled Caption Buttons. Look to the right and you'll see that the Size: title and white box below it have lit up. Watch the Minimize -, Maximize □, and Close ✕ buttons on the Inactive, Active, and Message Box bars as you click the up and down arrows to find the size of Caption Buttons that you like. Find the size you like and leave it.

Note: When you have a window open on your desktop you will see these symbols in the upper right-hand corner of the window, Minimize -, Restore 🗗 or Maximize □, and Close ✕. Take a moment and hold your pointer over each one of these symbols or buttons on the Control Panel window top title bar, you'll see - □ ✕, to view the tooltip for each one. To make a window fill your whole screen or Maximize it, click the □ button. To make a window so that it is the size that the Control Panel is right now, click the 🗗 button. To Minimize and place a window down on your bottom taskbar, click the - button. To completely Close or exit a window, click the ✕ button. When you Minimize a window and place it on the bottom taskbar, you will see a small box with the name of the window that you have minimized. To open it back up, just click once on the small box. Always check your bottom taskbar before shutting down your computer or when you're done working on it, to make sure that you haven't left any windows open and minimized.

If you open up a new window in the minimized view and it appears in a part of your screen that makes it hard to view or it is covering something that you want to see underneath it, here's how to move it. Move your pointer to the top title bar of the window that tells what this new window is, i.e. Control Panel. Click your mouse button and hold it down. Now move your pointer. The window will move with the pointer and you can position it on the screen so that is easier for you to see what is underneath it. Release the mouse button when you have it positioned where you want it.

If you don't see the − or □ buttons on the toolbar next to the ✖ button on a window toolbar, you won't be able to Minimize or Maximize that window. You can practice Minimizing, Restoring, and Maximizing windows when we work on projects later in the book.

-And now back to our task at hand. Find the next Item: below Caption Buttons called Desktop and click once on it to put it in the white box. The Color: title next to it will light up. The color you choose now will be the desktop background color. You will see it if you chose to Center a picture on the desktop. This color will also apply to the small colored boxes with text that are below the icons on the left-hand side of your desktop. For example: Below the icon that looks like a computer, you will see a colored box that says My Computer. Follow the previous steps to find your color. When you have decided, click the OK button to return to Display Properties.

-The next Item: below Desktop is Icon. Click once on Icon on the drop down menu to put it in the white box. To the right of Icon the Size: title and box will light up. The number you choose will determine the size of the colored box below the icons. I have found that I like to keep these colored boxes small. The reason being, that I want to see as much of my desktop picture as I can. I usually set the Size at 25. Try Size 25 and then click once on the Apply button. Look at the boxes below the icons. What do you think? If they are too small you can adjust the size again and click the Apply button again. Keep trying until you find the size that you like. Don't worry if the font size is too big, we'll be changing that in a minute.

-Next, go down to the Font: title. Do you want to use the same font in the icon boxes that you used on your Inactive, Active, and Message bars? If so, click on the down arrow to find that font and click once on it. If not, find another font to use and then click the Apply button. How does it look?

-You can now adjust the size of the font by clicking on the down arrow under Size: and picking the size you want. Click once on the Apply button to see what it will look like. Adjust it by trying different sizes until you find the size you like.

-The next Item: below Icon is Icon Spacing (Horizontal). Click once on it on the menu to put it in the white box. This item controls the horizontal space between each icon and colored icon box. I usually choose size 25. Again, a smaller distance horizontally between each icon allows me to view more of my desktop picture. Experiment with different size numbers and then click the Apply button each time to view how it will look. Leave it at the number you have decided on.

-Below Icon Spacing (Horizontal), you'll see Icon Spacing (Vertical). Click once on it to put it in the white box. Vertical spacing controls the vertical space between each icon and colored icon box. Experiment with the size as you did in the previous step for horizontal spacing. I usually keep mine set at 42.

-The next Item: is the Inactive Title Bar. Click once on it on the drop down menu to put it in the white box. You can either make this bar the same colors, font, font size, etc. as the Active Title Bar and Message Box or change it. Sometimes I like to use the same colors but change the order of them so that Color 2 is now the first Color. Sometimes I pick new colors that will correspond and compliment the Active and Message Box Bars. Experiment with colors, fonts, and font sizes. When you've decided how you want the Inactive Title Bar to look, go to the next Item.

-The Inactive Window Border was set when you chose the Size and Color for the Active Window Border. You can leave the settings as they are.

-The Item: below Inactive Window Border is Menu. Click once on it to put it in the white box. Watch the bar below the words Active Window as you experiment with Size: and Color:. You can choose a color for this bar that compliments the 3D objects color or use the same color as 3D objects. The color that you choose, now, will also be on the menu that pops up when you click the Start button in the lower left-hand corner of your screen. Choose the size, color, font, font size, and font color that you want this item to be. When you've chosen all of these things, click once on the Apply button. Then, take a moment and click once on the Start button so that you can check the Start menu to see how it looks with this color, font, font size, and font color. Make adjustments if you need to and then click the Apply button again to view the Start menu. When you have it set to your preference, go to the next Item on the drop down menu.

-Below Menu on the Item list is Message Box. Watch the word Message, below the Message Box Bar as you experiment with Font:, Size:, and Color:. Note: If you choose a color other than black, you will need to remember to change the color if you are working on a document or letter. For instance, choosing a dark blue will make that the automatic color for font whenever you are typing a letter or document. If you need to print out documents, you'll need to remember to change the font color to black if that is the standard color that you are used to. I usually leave the font color for Message Box set at black.

-Below Message Box on the Item list is Palette Title. I always leave this at Size: 19 and then choose the same font I have been using and the same size for font. As much as I've searched I still cannot find what Palette Title applies to. Oh well!

-Next on the Item list is Scrollbar. Click once on it to put it in the white box. You'll notice that the Size: title lights up with the up and down arrows. Experiment with different sizes and watch the scrollbar on the displayed Active Window. I've found that the scrollbar is much easier to use with the pointer if it is set at a higher number, i.e. size 21 or above. Experiment and find a size that you are comfortable with.

-Now, click once on Selected Items below Scrollbar on the drop down menu. Watch the space below the Active Window Bar as you use the up and down arrows under Size:. Choose the size that you like.

-Next to Size: is Color:. Whenever certain buttons are clicked in they will show this color. Also, when you highlight items on a menu or list they will be this color. For instance, on the Start Menu and on the lists: Item, Scheme, Font, and Size you highlighted different titles as you moved your pointer over them. This is the Selected Items color. I find that it is best to use a lighter shade of the color that I chose for the Menu.

-Now you can experiment with Font:, font Size:, and font Color:, or you can set them at the same font that you have been using all along.

-Tooltip is next on the drop down menu list. To find out what a Tooltip is, move your pointer up to the top right-hand corner of the Display Properties window to the ✖ button. Just keep your pointer there for a moment, but don't click. A little box will appear below it that says Close. Next, move your pointer to the left so that it is over the ❓ button. Leave it there for a moment, without clicking, and you will see a box appear below it that says Help. These little boxes are Tooltips. The color that you choose for the first Color: box will be the color inside the Tooltip box. Next, you can choose the Font:, font Color:, and font Size:.

-The last Item on the list is Window. The first Color: box will probably be white. This color determines the color of the page when you are working in Word, Works, Outlook Express, etc. You want a white color, but I've found that the plain white is really too bright and difficult to look at for long whenever I am composing a letter or other document. So, I use a color that is more of an eggshell color. You can experiment by clicking into the color box, clicking on the different brown color boxes and then moving the left pointing arrow next to the vertical shading box to the top where the color is almost white. Or, you can just leave it the white color it is now if it doesn't bother you.

-The second Color: box determines the color that your Window Text will be. See Window Text below Active Window. This color was set when you chose the font color for the Message Box text.

-Now, move your pointer down to the lower right-hand corner and click once on the Apply button.

-Next, move your pointer up to the button that says Save As…and click once. A new box will open up titled Save Scheme. Below that you will see Save this color scheme as:. You'll see a blinking bar inside the white box. Type in a name for your new color scheme in this box.

-I usually name my schemes to go with the desktop picture that I selected the colors for. For instance, I have a color scheme that coordinates with the Cloud wallpaper. So, I call that scheme Cloud Blue. When you've typed in your color scheme name, click the OK button once. Great! Now that scheme has been saved and all you have to do to use it again is find it in the Scheme: list, click once on it, and then click the Apply button! You can now close the Display Properties window and the Control Panel window by clicking on the Close buttons in the upper right-hand corners of each window.

Computer Screen Settings

Let's take a few moments to tweak some of your computer screen controls to your preference. Have you ever played with the brightness and contrast controls on your TV? If you're looking at any kind of screen and the brightness is too high, it can be very difficult look at. When I first got my computer the screen was very difficult for me to look at because the brightness was set much too high. We'll now be adjusting these controls on your computer screen. The settings that are in place may be just fine for you. If that is the case, then you won't need to change anything. Follow along anyway, though, so that you know where to find these settings in the future if you want to adjust them. We are also going to be adjusting the volume and checking your time and date settings.

Go to your desktop and look down to the right on the bottom taskbar. You'll see different icons lined up. Hold your pointer over each one for a moment so that you can see the tooltip for each one. Generally the icons that you will see are: a telephone with the tooltip Modem is not in use, a speaker with the tooltip Volume, a computer screen with the tooltip Screen and sound control, and probably others as well. When you are connected to the Internet, you will also see two little connected computer screens that will light up when you are sending/receiving email messages, going to a different website on the Internet, or downloading information from a website. You'll also see the present time.

-Click once on the speaker icon, with the tooltip Volume, and a little Volume box will pop up. You'll see a little slider bar. Place your pointer over it and then click and hold your mouse button as you move it up and down. This will adjust the volume of the sounds that you hear on your computer. This feature is especially useful if you are visiting a website that plays music and you want to adjust the volume. If you don't want to listen to the music, you can slide the bar all the way down to Mute.

-If you don't see the computer screen icon on your bottom taskbar, with the tooltip Screen and sound control, there's another way to find it. Click your Start button, move your pointer up to Settings, and then click once on Control Panel. We've done this before, remember? Find and double click on, Display, to open up the Display Properties window. Next, find and click once on the Settings tab. Look towards the bottom right of the window, find and click once on the Advanced...button to open up another window. Find and click once on the Monitor controls tab and then follow along with the screen control steps that I will be covering in a moment.

-If you do see the computer screen icon on your bottom toolbar, with the tooltip Screen and sound control, put your pointer over it and click once. A menu will pop up with the titles Advanced Display, Advanced Sound, Show Quick Controls, and Exit. Click once on Advanced Display to open up the Monitor Properties window.

-Under Monitor Controls look for Screen Brightness and Screen Contrast. Take some time and slowly move each of the down pointing sliding arrows, under these two titles, in either direction. Remember to hold your pointer over the arrow, click and hold your mouse button, and then move your mouse. Watch your computer screen as you do this. Is there a setting that you prefer to the default setting? Leave the arrows at the settings you have chosen.

-Find and click once on the Done button in the bottom right-hand corner of this window and then the Close button in the upper right-hand corner to close this window. If you want to, you can take some time and explore the other settings and experiment with them. Generally, these are fine as they are with the default settings. If you do experiment with them, remember where the original setting was so that you can leave it at the original default setting. Great! If you did need to adjust the brightness and contrast, like I did, your screen will be much easier to look at now.

-Place your pointer over the time. A tooltip will come up that tells you today's date. To set your preferences in the Date/ Time window, right click your mouse if you are right-handed or left click your mouse if you are left-handed once. Find and click once on Adjust Date/ Time on the menu that pops up. This will open up the Date/ Time Properties window.

-Check the date and time to make sure they are correct. If you need to adjust the date or AM/PM just use the up and down arrows to adjust them. Now, look under Time Zone. What time zone do you live in? You can click on the down arrow to view the Time Zone list. When you find the time zone that you live in, click once on it to put it in the white box.

-Below this, you will see Automatically adjust clock for daylight saving changes with a white box to the left of it. If you want this automatically done for you, click in the white box to check it. When you've made your choices, click once on the Apply button in the lower right-hand corner and then the OK button.

Let's Personalize Your Mouse

Did you know that you could set preferences for how you want your mouse pointer and cursor to look and behave? You can! Let's do it now.

-First, open up your Control Panel window by clicking once on the Start button, moving up to Settings, and then clicking once on Control Panel. Find and double click on Mouse in your Control Panel list to open up the Mouse Properties window. Have you ever wondered why they call it a Mouse? So have I. I guess it does kind of look like mouse with a tail.

-You'll see three tabs with the titles Buttons, Pointers, and Motion. Make sure you are in the Buttons window. Are you left-handed or right-handed? Make sure that the white circle next to your preference is checked.

-Do you find it hard to double click quickly? Many people do. You can set the double click speed low if you have a hard time double clicking quickly. To adjust to your preference, move the sliding, down pointing arrow towards Slow. To the right of this you'll see Test area:. Below that you'll see a small jack-in-the-box. You can test the double clicking slowness of your mouse by double clicking on the small jack-in-the-box. If Jack doesn't pop out of the box when you double click on top of the box, you need to set the speed slower. When he pops up after you double click, you know that you've set the speed at the setting that is right just for you.

-Next, click once on the Pointers tab. The first title will be Schemes. Click once on the down arrow next to the box below this title to view the Schemes list. Take a few moments to click once on each of the schemes in the list. This will place the scheme that you clicked on in the white box. Watch the viewing area below. This viewing area will show you how the different pointers look in that scheme. You can use the down arrow or scroll bar to view the whole list if you want to. Which Scheme did you like the most? I like my pointers to be large so that I can see them easily, so usually I use the Windows Standard (extra large) Scheme. When you've decided which scheme you want to use, click once on it so that it is in the white box.

-Next, click on the Motion tab. You'll see Pointer speed and Pointer trail. Do you want your pointer to move fast, slow, or in between across your screen? I really can't tell much difference between slow and fast, so I usually just leave the speed in between slow and fast. Do you want your pointer to leave a trail as it moves across the screen? Set your preferences.

-When you've made all of your Mouse choices click once on the Apply button in the lower right corner and then the OK button. You've just personalized your Mouse!

Events and Their Sounds

Have you noticed that, whenever you do different things on your computer, it makes a sound? Your computer came with default sounds for different events. For instance, you hear different sounds when you minimize or maximize a window, when you receive new email messages, or when you click on something you shouldn't (mine does this frequently.) Did you know that you could change the default settings for these sounds? You can. Let's experiment with this option.

-In your Control Panel window, find and double click on Sounds on the list to open up the Sounds Properties window.

-The first title that you will see will be Events:. Below this, you'll see a list of different events that occur in Windows, Power Management, Windows Explorer, Media Player, etc. For now we are going to concentrate on the events in Windows and Windows Explorer. Scroll back up to the top of the list and find Windows. To the left of certain events you'll see the speaker icon. That means that these events have a sound accompanying them. Click on the first event you see that has a speaker next to it.

-You'll notice that under Sound and Name a title will appear in the white box. Next to the name a Preview box will show the icon for that name. To the right of the Preview box, you'll see a right pointing arrow. When you click once on the right pointing arrow, you will hear the sound that is set for that event. Take a few moments and preview or listen to the sounds for the different events listed under Windows.

-Click back on the first event under Windows that has a speaker next to it. Now, find and click once on the Browse button below the Name box to open up the Browse for...window. You'll see a list of different sounds to choose from, if you want to change a sound for a particular event.

-Take a few moments and click on each of the sound titles in the list. As you click on each one, look below and find Preview with the right pointing arrow next to it. Click on the right pointing arrow each time you click on a title to preview or hear what that sound sounds like.

-When you have previewed all of the sounds, find and click once on the Close button in the upper right-hand corner to go back to the Sounds Properties window.

-Now, go back and click on each event under Windows and preview the sound again. Do you like the sound or would you like to change it? For instance, let's say that you don't like the sound for Maximize and want to change it.

-Click on Maximize in the list to put the current sound in the Name box. Next, click on the Browse button to open the window where you can choose which sound you now want to use.

-Look through the list and find and click once on the sound title that you would now like to use for Maximize. This will put the title in the File name: box. Find and click once on the OK button to return to the Sounds Properties, window.

-Now, go through the list and decide if you want to change any of the other sounds.

-Next, scroll down the Events list and find Empty Recycle Bin under Windows Explorer. Listen to the assigned sound and decide if you would like to leave it as is or change it. You can play around with the rest of the sound events if you want to, we've just covered some of the major ones.

-When you're done changing the sounds that you wanted to change, click once on the Apply button at the bottom of the window and then once on the OK button.

Your computer will now have sounds that are pleasing to you. One of my favorites is Utopia Windows Exit. I have this sound set to go with the New Mail Notification. Now, whenever a new message arrives in my Outlook Express inbox, I hear this delightful little giggle! It always makes me smile.

Congratulations, you've just personalized your computer and made it very visually appealing and fun to hear by applying colors and options that you love! Looking at the same picture day after day can be boring, though. Just as you probably rearrange your furniture, pictures, and accessories from time to time, you can rearrange your computer from time to time. Now that you know how to set up your own person-alized schemes, you can make more. Was there another Background Wallpaper that you liked besides the one you picked? Maybe you liked several or all of them. Take some time to make color schemes that will go with the other wallpapers that you liked. Just go back to the begin-ning of this chapter and follow the steps to apply a new wallpaper and personalized color scheme. Soon, you'll be a pro and won't need to refer to the directions at all.

Finding and Saving New Wallpapers

Now that you know how to change the wallpapers for your desktop and personalize your own color scheme, how about finding more wallpapers to add to your collection? If you're like me, you like a wide variety of pictures to choose from. There are many websites on the Internet where you can find free wallpapers. Searching for them is easy, but finding the perfect ones for you will probably take a little time. So, if you are planning on doing searches for new wallpapers, pick a time when you can view, at your leisure, all of the images at these different sites. Most sites are set up with wallpaper categories, i.e. Animals, Nature scenes, etc. Wallpapers are generally made in JPEG format, which is a compressed file format. The nice thing about this is that it keeps the image file size small and won't use up a lot of space on your hard drive when you save them to your computer. So, you can have lots of them!

I've set up a special wallpaper folder in the My Document folder, where I keep the wallpaper images that I've found on the Internet and saved. Let's go ahead and do this now so that you will have it ready to go when you find new wallpapers on the Internet. Setting up this wallpaper folder will help you to keep your images organized.

-Find the My Documents icon shortcut on your desktop. Remember the icons run down the left side of the screen. When you've found the icon, double click on it to open up the My Documents window. It will say My Documents on the top title bar of the window. If you don't have a My Documents icon on your desktop, along with the other icons, you can access it by double clicking on the My Computer icon on your desktop. Then double click on (C:) to open up that window. Find and double click on My Documents on the list to open up this window.

-Find and click once on the File button on the far left side of the top toolbar. Move your pointer down the menu that pops down and highlight New. Then, slide your pointer over to the new menu and click once on Folder.

-Look in the window file area and you'll see a that a new folder icon titled New Folder has been added to the list. If the New Folder title is highlighted and in a little box, go to the next step. If the New Folder title is not highlighted, hold your pointer over it and right click your mouse if you are right-handed or left click if you are left-handed. A new menu will pop up. Look towards the bottom of this small menu and then find and click once on Rename.

-You'll notice that the New Folder title is now highlighted and in a little box. Hit the Delete key on your keyboard once to remove this title. Now you'll see a little box with a blinking bar. Let's name this new folder Wallpapers. Type in your new folder name and then hit the Enter key on your keyboard once. Now when you find wallpapers on the Internet, you can put them in this new folder.

When you've found images on the Internet that you would like to use, read the website directions carefully because they can vary at different websites. Picking new images for wallpaper is usually pretty easy. Typically, all you have to do is click once on the thumbnail of the image, which is just a small picture of the image. Once you do, you'll go to the web page that has a larger picture. Then, you'll be instructed to choose a screen size. To find out your screen area size, click once on the Settings tab in the Display Properties window (remember that the Display Properties window is the one we worked in to change the color scheme, etc., of your computer.) Towards the bottom of the window on the right, you'll see Screen area. Below this title will be your screen area size. For instance, my screen size is 800 by 600 pixels. So, whenever I save desktop wallpaper that I have found on the Internet, I choose the 800 x 600 download size.

If you want to save the image in the new Wallpapers folder that we just set up so that you can use it again, you will need to follow the website directions and click on Save image as…. When you right click on the image, you'll see this title on the small menu that pops up. Some websites will tell you to click on Set as wallpaper…when you right click on an image. If you do this, the image will only be set on your desktop temporarily and it won't be saved to your hard drive. So, to save it, make sure that you click once on Save image as…. The following directions are for future reference when you are saving an image to your Wallpapers folder.

-A new Save Picture window will open up after you have clicked once on Save image as…. Make sure it says My Documents in the white box next to Save in:. If it doesn't, you can click the Up folder icon with the up arrow to get to (C:). The Up folder icon is next to the Save in: white box and when you hold your pointer over it for a moment you'll see the tooltip Up One Level.

-When it says (C:) in the Save in: white box look down and find My Documents on the list. Double click on My Documents to open it up.

-Then, find and double click on the Wallpapers folder. Your Wallpapers window will now be open.

-If you want to change the name of the wallpaper you are saving to one you will remember, just click once in the File name: white box, delete the name that is there, and type in a new name. If you have clicked in the white box at the beginning of the file name, hit the Delete key on your keyboard to remove the name. If you have clicked in the white box at the end of the file name, hit the Backspace key on your keyboard to delete the file name.

-Then, click once on the Save button to save this wallpaper to the Wallpaper folder. Click once on the Close button to close this window.

-If you want to check and make sure that the wallpaper has been saved to this folder, double click on the My Documents icon on your desktop. The My Documents window will open up.

-Double click on the Wallpaper folder that you saved the wallpaper in to open it up. Click once on the wallpaper title and a description, file size, and small preview of the image will be on the left side of this window, if your window has been set up to be viewed as a web page.

-If yours hasn't been set up to be viewed as a web page and you would like to be able to see a small preview of the wallpaper, click once on the View button on the top toolbar. Find as Web Page on the menu and click once on it to put a check next to it. You should now be able to see a small preview and description on the left side of this window. And, now you know for sure that it is saved in this folder and you will be able to follow the directions for applying wallpaper to your desktop.

Here's a quick way to access your Display Properties window, if you want to change the wallpaper background and appearance. Place your pointer over the picture that is now on your desktop. Now, right click if you're right-handed or left click if you're left-handed. A small menu will pop up. Look for Properties at the bottom of this menu and click once on it. Presto! There's your Display Properties window.

To apply a new wallpaper image to your desktop that you have found and put in your new Wallpapers folder, follow the directions given below.

-Right click once anywhere on the current desktop picture.

-A small menu will pop up. Move your pointer down the menu and find Properties at the bottom. Click once on it.

-A new window will open titled Display Properties. Make sure you are in the Background tab window.

-Find the Browse button, in the middle right of the window, and click once on it.

-A new window will open up titled Open. Click the folder icon with the up arrow, next to the Look in: white box and with the tooltip Up One Level, until it says (C:) in the white box next to Look in:.

-Find the folder that is titled, My Documents, in the list in the large white area and double click on it. This will put it in the white box next to Look in:.

-Find the folder in the large white area titled, Wallpapers, and double click on it.

-Click once on the wallpaper that you would now like to have on your desktop.

-Click once on the Open button. The image should now be on the small computer screen in the Display Properties window.

-Find and click once on the Apply button in the bottom right corner of this window. Your image should now be on the desktop. Click once on the OK button to close the Display Properties window.

*　　*　　*　　*　　*　　*

Here are some addresses for sites where you can search for free wallpaper images, Photobreak at photobreak.com, Beautiful Wallpapers at beautifulwallpapers.com, Snap Shot at snap-shot.com, Wallpapers at wallpapers.com, Ace Wallpapers at acewallpapers.com, and Top Downloads at topdownloads.net.

These six websites are a good place to start looking for desktop wallpaper images. If you want to do a broader search for wallpaper images, I've listed other search sites and ways to search at the end of the Having Fun with Desktop Themes chapter. Through out my book, I will be providing you with different website addresses. Always be sure to put www. before any of the website addresses that I provide for you.

I like to change my desktop picture and personalized scheme about every 1-2 weeks. I really look forward to choosing which one I'll display next. We're going to cover Screensavers next, so go and get a cup of coffee or cool drink and take break. You deserve it! You've been working hard and learning fun and valuable skills that will help you with all of the Windows programs.

3

Inspiring Screen Savers

Do you like your screen saver? Is yours customized? I have a great time personalizing my screen savers and changing them occasionally. We're going to spend time in this chapter exploring the screen savers that are installed on your computer and then set up some special ones just for you to use and rotate.

There is a list of screen savers on your computer that we will experiment with in a moment. But first, I want to share with you why I love coming back to my computer when I've been away from it for a bit. I enjoy surrounding myself with positive and inspirational thoughts. This is because I believe that words, as well as colors, have a powerful affect on us. Now, I can see these inspiring words when I come back to my computer after being away from it for awhile because my screen savers have these inspiring words on them. Take a few moments and think of words, phrases, and thoughts that inspire you or that make you smile. Do you have a favorite author that you quote often? Maybe a fortune cookie message really caught your attention. Go to your bookcase and start looking or think up some inspiring or fun phrases of your own!

Here are a few of my favorites:

* Shoot for the Moon! Even if you miss you will still Land in the Stars! (Les Brown)
* All My Hard Work Will Soon Pay Off!
* I Deserve the Best.
* I Can Have My Dreams!
* I Live in Beauty.
* I Am Grateful.
* I am Special!
* I Accept and Receive Loving Abundance.
* I Open My Heart To Give and Receive with Love.
* I Am Creative!
* I Send Thoughts of Love and Unity into the World.

Recently, I set up a new computer for a friend. She liked my little Astro so much that she bought one just like it. Being that she was a beginner, too, I told her I would set up her new computer for her and make it visually appealing for her. I had a blast! When I set up her screensaver, I put in the message: Mari is Very Special!! She was delighted when she saw it and still uses it. I like to believe that it helps in some small way. So, think about what words would help you. Open up and use your imagination. Let yourself be creative and free. This is your computer and you have a right to personalize it so that it will help and inspire you.

3D Text Screen Saver

-When you've thought of several inspiring thoughts click once on the Start button, move your pointer up to Settings and then across to Control Panel and click once.

-Find Display in the list and double click on it to open up the Display Properties window. Click once on the Screen Saver tab.

-You'll once again see an image of your computer monitor. Below the image you'll see Screen Saver. Click the down arrow to view the list of screen savers.

-Move the cursor bar up or click the up arrow until you reach the top of the list. When you see 3D Text, highlight it with your pointer and click once on it. It should now be in the box below Screen Saver.

-To the right of this box you will see a button that says Settings. Click on it once to open up a new window called 3D Text Setup.

-Below this you'll see Display with two items, Text and Time, beneath it. Click once in the small white circle that is to the left of Text. A white box will light up to the right of Text. Click once inside it. When you see the blinking bar, type in your inspiring words!

-Below Time you'll see Size with the words Small and Large beneath it. Place your pointer over the elongated down arrow, hold your mouse button down, and move the arrow all the way to Large. Release the mouse button. This will put your inspiring or fun message in large letters as it moves across your screen.

-Next, go to Resolution where you'll see Min and Max. Move the down arrow again as you did before all the way to Max.

-Take a moment and review your Font page in the back of the book. What font would you like to use for your inspirational message? Next, look to the far right side of the window and you'll see a button that says Choose Font…. Click once on this button and a new window will open up called Font. Under the title Font: click the up and down arrows until you find the font that you would like to use. When you've found the font that you want to use, click once on it. A sample viewing of the font can be seen in the box below Sample.

-Depending on the font that you chose you may be able to choose a Font Style:. If you see Regular and then Bold under this title, you can choose which style you would like applied to your font. Click on each one to see how your font will look in the Sample box. When you've made your choices click once on the OK button. This will return you to the 3D Text Setup window.

-Now let's experiment a little bit. Under the title Surface Style, you'll see Solid Color and Textured. Click once in the little white circle to the left of Solid Color. This is an interesting setting because although the color seems set on the surface of the font, it slowly changes color. To see this happening, click once on the OK button to go back to the Screen Saver window.

-Watch the small monitor screen. To see what it will look like on your screen, click the button that says Preview. After you do this take your hand off of your mouse. In the Preview screen you can see the Screen Saver as long as you don't move the mouse. Watch the colors change on your inspiring words. When you've previewed it for as long as you need to, move your mouse and you will return to the Screen Saver window.

-Now, click once on the Settings button again to take you back to the 3D Text Setup window. Click once in the little white circle to the left of Textured. Next, click the button that says Texture. This will take you to the Choose Texture File window.

-Under the large white box, you'll see a left arrow, a right arrow, and a scroll bar. Move your mouse pointer over the scroll bar, click, and then hold your mouse button down. Move the bar to the right, or you can just click the right pointing arrow. When you see the title 1st boot you've reached the texture files. The following files would make interesting textures for the surface of your font. 1st boot, Blue Rivets, Clouds, Forest, Gold Weave, Sandstone, Stitches, Straw Mat, and Waves. These are the wallpapers that you saw when choosing a Desktop Background.

-To choose one of the files, click once on it so that it is highlighted. Then click the button below that says Open.

-Click the OK button in the 3D Text Setup window. You'll now be able to view your texture choice on the small monitor screen. Click once on the Preview button, if you want to see it on your large screen. If you want to view some of the other texture files, repeat these steps by clicking once on the Settings button to take you back to the 3D Text setup window.

-So what did you decide? Do you want your inspiring words to be a solid color that changes color or with a special colored texture? Which one really caught your attention? I personally like the Cloud texture and the Solid color so I alternate them. Make your choice by clicking in the white circle next to Solid Color or Textured. If you picked Textured, make sure that you have selected the texture file that you liked the best.

-Now that you've decided on the font and how it will look there are a few more choices. Under Solid Color and Textured, in the 3D Text Setup window, you'll see Speed and below that Slow and Fast. I have found that putting the down arrow all the way to Slow makes it easier to read. Experiment a little bit with the Speed option. You may like having your message move more quickly around your screen. To see the different speeds you want to try, set the arrow at a point between Slow and Fast, then click the OK button in the 3D Text setup window to go back to the Screen Saver window. You'll be able to view the speed you've chosen on the small monitor screen or preview it on your large screen. Click Settings again to try another speed. Leave the arrow set at the speed that you liked the best.

-Under Speed you'll see Spin Style. Click once on the down arrow to view the list. Take a few minutes to experiment with None, See-Saw, Wobble, and Random. Click on an item to highlight it and then click once on the OK button to see what it does by watching the small monitor screen or previewing the large screen in the Screen Saver window. Click once on Settings to return to the 3D Text Setup window.

-Choose which Spin Style you would like for your inspiring phrase and then click once on the OK button to return to the Screen Saver window. Below the Settings...and Preview buttons, you'll see Wait:, a small white box with little up and down arrows, and then minutes. How long do you want the screen on your computer to be unattended before your screen saver comes on your screen? 5 minutes? 10? I've got mine set at 15 minutes. Make your choice by clicking on the up and down buttons.

-Once you've made your choice, click once on the Apply button in the lower right-hand corner of the Screen Saver window. This new screen saver is now set! You can use it now or later. If you want to change the saying you used for the 3D Text screensaver at a later date, just follow the previous steps.

Scrolling Marquee Screen Saver

Let's try another fun screen saver that you can use to input your inspiring thoughts.

-In the Screen Saver window under Screen Saver, click the down arrow to view the list again. When you find Scrolling Marquee, highlight it and click once on it so that it now appears in the box.

-Click the Settings…button next to Scrolling Marquee to go to the Options for Scrolling Marquee window. Near the bottom left-hand corner you'll see Background Color: with a color box beneath it and a down arrow. Click the down arrow to view the color choices.

-How do you want your background to look? A dark background will make your message really stand out, if you choose a light color for your font. Perhaps, you'd prefer more subtle shades. View the list and then highlight your choice for a background color and click once on it so that it now appears in the color box.

-Under Background Color: you'll see Text:. Click once in the white box next to Text: and type in your inspiring or fun message.

-Find the button that says Format Text…in the lower right-hand corner and click once on it.

-You are now in the Format Text window. Under Font:, you'll see a white box with a down arrow. Click the arrow to view the list. What type of font do you want for your new message? Perhaps a fun one, like

Juice ITC or Kristen, or an elegant one, like Vivaldi or Kunstler. Make your choice, highlight the font, and click once on it so that it now appears in the white box.

-Next, go to Font style:. You'll see a number of choices. Take a moment and click on each one. Below this you'll be able to see a Sample box. It will show you a view of your font and will change each time you choose a different font style. Which one do you like best? When you've found the font style that you like, leave it highlighted.

-Size: is next to Font style. In the white box below it will be different numbers for different sizes of text. I always set mine to 72, which is the largest size. Click once on the size that you would like to use.

-Next, go to Effects. You'll see Strikeout and Underline with white boxes to the left of them. Strikeout puts a line through the center of your text. Underline does just that, it underlines your text. Click in each box to view in the Sample box what each one will look like. To leave an effect in, leave the check mark in the box. Maybe you don't want either. To remove an effect click again in the white box and the check will be removed.

-Under Color:, you'll see another color box with a down arrow. Click the down arrow to view the list. Choose the color that you want for your font, highlight it, and click once on it to put it in the color box.

-Under Script:, leave it set at Western. Find the OK button and click once on it, to return to the Options for Scrolling Marquee window.

-Find Position in the upper left-hand corner. You'll see Centered and Random, with small white circles to the left of them. If you choose Centered, your message will always scroll through the center of your screen. If you choose Random, it will scroll randomly through different parts of your screen. Which would you prefer? Click in the white circle to the left of the one you've chosen.

-Finally, find Speed. At what speed do you want your message to scroll across the screen? You can experiment by setting the speed and then clicking the OK button to view or preview how it will look. To return to the Options for Scrolling Marquee window, click Settings.

Once you've made your choice, click the OK button to return to the Screen Saver window.

 -If your message is set and you like the way it looks, click once on the Apply button in the lower right-hand corner.

* * * * * *

 Fantastic! You've just added two more personalized and visually appealing features to your computer. Now when you return to your computer, after leaving it unattended for a few minutes, you'll see your own personalized message to yourself. Inspiring thoughts will be visually imprinted into your consciousness. You'll remember these thoughts in color!

 Which one would you like on your computer right now? The inspiring phrase you put in 3D Text or the one you put in Scrolling Marquee? Find it in the Screen saver list, click once on it to put in the box, click once on the Apply button, and then the OK button. That's it!

 Anytime you want to change your screen saver just find it on the list, highlight it, click once on it, and then click once on the Apply button. When you're ready for some new inspiring or fun messages on your screen saver, just follow the previous steps to input them and apply them. There are other screen savers that you can experiment with on the list, also. With the rest of them, though, you won't be able to input words. Some have features that you can alter. Take a few minutes to acquaint yourself with the other screen savers on the list.

 If you'd like to experiment with more screen savers, all you have to do is search. You can find just about anything on the Internet, including screen savers. Like Desktop themes and wallpapers they are usually free. Because screen savers are generally large files, they are compressed when put on a website. In order for you to open the screen saver, once it is downloaded, you will need an unzip utility. At the end of the Desktop Themes chapter, I've listed some websites to visit where you can find all of these things. You can search for screen savers at these sites, also. Or, you can just continue to use the two you now have installed and rotate inspiring and fun sayings. It's up to you!

4

Having Fun With Desktop Themes

To see if you have Desktop Themes Plus! installed on your computer click once on the Start button, move your pointer up to Settings, across to Control Panel, and then click once to open up this window. Read through the list to see if you can find Desktop Themes. If you see it on your list, it has been installed. If you don't see it, you can install it by finding Add/ Remove Programs, which is on this same Control Panel list, and double clicking on it to open up this window.

Next, find and click once on the Windows Setup tab. It will take a moment for it to search for the installed components. Look for Desktop themes on the list. Click in the white box to the left of Desktop Themes to put a check in it, and then click once on the Details…button that is near the bottom of this window. Read the directions at the top of this window. If the white boxes next to each of the themes don't have checks in them, take a moment and click once in these boxes to select them. When you've done this, click once on the OK button to close this window. Now you'll be back in the Add/ Remove Programs and the Windows Setup tab window. If you checked all of the boxes in the Desktop Themes window to install all of the themes listed, under Description near the bottom of the window it will say 17 of 17 components selected. Click once on the Apply button at the bottom right of this window and then click once on the Close button. This will install themes on your computer.

If you find at a later date that you don't want all of the themes installed you can always go back and uncheck the specific themes that you don't want installed. This will free up disc space. For now, though, go ahead and install them all, if they haven't already been installed, so that you can see what they look like.

* * * * * *

It's time to personalize your computer some more! The wonderful thing about having Desktop Themes Plus! on your computer is that you can install desktop themes that you find on the Internet. Also, you have more desktop images to choose from in the themes list, along with the desktop wallpaper pictures. I have found that sometimes I don't care for some of the colors, fonts, icons, etc. that have been made to go with the main image in a theme. With Themes Plus!, you can adjust and change the theme to look just the way you want it to look. Each theme usually comes with sounds, also, for the different events that occur on your computer, like maximizing a window or emptying your trash can. Again, you don't have to use the sounds that have been set up with a particular Theme if you don't like them.

There are a lot of websites set up that have desktop themes for you to download and usually they are free. At the end of this chapter I'll go over how to search for themes and provide you with some websites to check out. You will need an unzip utility if you choose to download most desktop themes off of the Internet, though. I have found one website that sets up their desktop themes in a different format so that you won't need an unzip utility. I'll include website addresses for these places, also. When you visit these websites, be sure to read the instructions that they have available on how to install their themes.

I have two Dolphin themes that I love and a beautiful theme made from a painting done by one of my favorite artists. I'm still searching for

Angel themes, because I really haven't found any that I like yet. I'm always on the lookout for themes that are visually appealing to me. I love it when someone sees my computer and says, "Wow! What a beautiful picture!" Lucky me, I get to look at them every day!

-Okay, let's get started. Open up your Control Panel by first clicking once on the Start button. Move your cursor up to Settings and then across to Control Panel and click once. Find Desktop Themes on the list and double click on it to open up your Desktop Themes window.

-Find the white box with a down arrow next to Theme:. Click the down arrow to view the list. We're going to start with one that I like.

-Move the cursor bar and scroll down until you see Underwater (high color). Highlight it with your pointer and click once on it to put it in the white box.

-Your preview window should now show a new image. Look to the right of this window and find Settings. Under Settings you'll see Screen saver, Sound events, Mouse pointers, Desktop wallpaper, Icons, Colors, Font names and styles, and Font and window sizes. Each title will have a white box to the left. Click once inside each box to check it, if it doesn't already have a check.

-Now, go up to the Screen saver button and click once on it to preview the screen saver that goes with this theme. Move your mouse when you are ready to return to the Desktop Theme window.

-Next, click once on the Settings button. A new window titled Preview Underwater (high color) will open up. There will be three tabs in this window titled Pointers, Sounds, and Visuals. Click once on the Pointers tab.

-You'll see Mouse pointer type: and large white box with a list. Click once on each title to see what the pointer will look like in the Preview box below.

-Next, click once on the Sounds tab. Under Sound event:, you'll see another list. Click on each title and then click the button below with the right pointing arrow to hear what the sound will be for that event.

-Now, click on the Visuals tab. You've already seen the Wallpaper bitmap and Screen saver on the Visual element list. Click once on the other titles to preview what that icon will look like in the preview box below. These are the icons that will be on your desktop if you choose to keep them. They will replace the ones you now have. Now, close the Preview Underwater window, by clicking the Close button in the upper right-hand corner, to return to the Desktop Theme window.

Let's say that you've decided that you like this theme, too. You want to rotate it as one of your desktop themes and use it at some point in the future. The one Setting that you have to have checked if you decide you want to use this theme is the Desktop wallpaper. All of the other settings are optional. Which settings did you like and not like? Uncheck, by clicking in the white boxes, the boxes of the settings that you didn't like.

For instance, let's say that you have decided not to keep the colors, fonts, styles, and window sizes and would like to personalize your own. You would then...

-Click once on the Apply button. Now, close the Desktop theme window. Look in the Control Panel window list for Display and double click on it.

-In the Display Properties window, click once on the Appearance tab and personalize a color scheme just as you did earlier in the book to go with this new Underwater desktop image. When you've created your new personalized color scheme click once on the Apply button.

-Save your new color scheme with a name that you will remember in case you want to use it with another image as you did earlier in the book. Close the Display Properties window.

-Then, open the Desktop Theme window by double clicking on it in the Control Panel list. Near the top of the window you'll see Theme:, with a white box and down arrow next to it. To the right of the white box find and click once on the Save as...button. A new Save Theme window will open up.

-Near the bottom of the window you'll see File name: with a white box next to it. Inside the white box, you'll see untitled highlighted with a blinking bar. Hit the Delete key on your keyboard to clear untitled and then type in a name for the theme you have just created. For instance, if you decided to personalize a new theme for Underwater, you could name it My Underwater. Now, click once on the Save button. Your new personalized theme is now saved and listed with the other desktop themes. If you decide to use it in the future, you can just click on the theme name you chose and then click once on the Apply button.

If you chose to use the desktop icons that go with the Underwater theme, those icons will now look different on your desktop. What if you have decided you want to change them back to the original icons? You can do it quickly and easily by double clicking on Display in the Control Panel list. Now, click once on the Effects tab. You'll see the icons in the white box. If you want to change the icon back to the original, click once on it to highlight it and then click once on the Default Icon button.

Take some time and preview the other themes that have been installed. If there are ones that you know for sure you'll never use, you can uninstall them. Follow the directions at the beginning of this chapter if you would like to do this.

When you've explored and experimented and are done, decide which theme you want on your computer right now. If you want to use a theme that you have personalized, find it in the drop down menu next to Theme: in the Desktop Themes window. Click once on it so that it is now in the box and then click once on the Apply button. If you don't see it in the drop down menu list, click on Other…to open up the Open Theme window. Find and click once on it to put it in the File name: box and then click once on the Open button. It will now be in the white box next to Theme: and you can click on the Apply button. You're set! Now, close this window by clicking once on the Close button. You can use this theme for as long as you like. When you're ready for a change, you can apply another theme.

Or, maybe you want to use the wallpaper background and color scheme that you set up earlier. If so, open up the Display window and apply the wallpaper picture that you liked. Then click once on the Appearance tab and apply the color scheme that you set up to go with this image.

Additional Desktop Themes

Now, what about finding additional themes for your computer? As I stated before, you can download free desktop themes off of the Internet. Keep in mind that desktop themes are generally large files. You'll want to watch how much memory you are using on your hard drive, if you download a lot of themes. Because graphics files are generally large and a theme usually has quite a few files in it, the theme designer zips them up so that the file is smaller and compressed. You will need an unzip utility to open them once you have downloaded them.

If you don't already have an unzip utility, you can find unzip utilities at ZDNet. Their address is zdnet.com. When you get to their website, find the search box and type in, free unzip utility, and then click the search button. If they have any free unzip utilities, a new webpage will show you that information. If you can't find any free ones, type unzip utility in the search box to look for ones they might have for sale. Generally they aren't very expensive and it is a good utility to have, as you might need it to unzip other files that you download off of the Internet. Check out, also, this website that has a free unzip utility. It's called Enzip at cpam.freeserve.co.uk. One of the best unzip utilities on the market is WinZip. You can find more information about it at winzip.com.

If you have decided you would like to have an unzip utility on your computer, be sure to read the directions carefully when downloading. Once you have downloaded this utility you'll be able to find it on your Programs menu. Click once on the Start button, move your pointer up to Programs, and then across to the menu. When you find the utility, there should be an arrow pointing to a smaller menu. Look for a Readme.txt or Help manual and click on them so that you can learn how to use this utility.

To search for desktop themes, wallpapers, screensavers, etc., on the Internet you can go to any search site to start your search. My favorite search sites are msn.com, yahoo.com, metacrawler.com, and snap.com. (Be sure to put www. before any of the website addresses that I provide for you in this book, when you type them in your browser address box.) Type desktop theme in the search box on their main page and click the search button. A new page will open up with listings for websites. Read through the information given for each one. If one sounds interesting, you can click on the name and it will take you right to that website.

Another way to search, that I really like, is to surf Webrings. Webrings are linked websites that have a common interest or subject for their websites. For instance, if you are searching for desktop themes, you can go to the main directory and type desktop themes in the search box. A new web page will open up that will list all of the webrings that have desktop themes. You can pick one of the webrings and begin surfing all of the websites in that ring.

When you go to a website that belongs to a webring, look for the desktop theme webring box that that has the words Next, Previous, Skip, and Home. You can click once on any of these words and your browser will take you to other similar websites. If you click on Next, you'll be taken to the next website in that ring. If you click on Previous, you'll be taken to the website that is right before the one you are now visiting. If you click on Home, you'll be taken to the website that lists, with descriptions, all of the websites in that particular webring. RingSurf, the webring Directory's website to search for different webrings, is at ringsurf.com.

Many websites have a Links page. If you see a button on a website that is titled Links, click on it to go to the web page that will list other websites that are similar in content or that have related subjects to the one you are visiting.

Here are a few addresses for websites that have desktop themes to get you started, Tucows at tucows.com, Tooties Theme Shop at tootsies-themeshop.com, Theme World at themeworld.com, and Desktop Reflections at desktopreflections.com. Look for a button on their web-site that says Desktop Themes and click on it to go to that web page. Next, is the address for a website that sets their desktop themes up in a different format, Themecloud 9 at themecloud9.com. You don't need an unzip utility to install their desktop themes. Most websites provide instructions for installing the themes. If you have any questions, you can email them for more information.

When you download desktop themes off of the Internet, they may not have all of the sounds and visuals that you saw and heard with the themes already installed on your computer. Sometimes they have screen savers or a combination of screen savers or no screen savers at all. It just depends on what the theme maker has decided to include with their theme.

Anytime you download anything off of the Internet you always need to be careful. Make sure that you have a good anti virus program installed on your computer. If I am downloading something from a large and well-known outfit like ZDNet or Microsoft, I, of course, don't worry. If I'm planning on downloading something from a small website and I'm not sure, I always email them and ask if all of their downloads have been scanned. Typically, they have been because the website owner usually downloads the theme onto their computer before putting it on their website, if the website is a compilation of other designer's themes. It never hurts to ask, though.

Your computer probably has a Download folder to put downloaded files into. Remember this whenever you download something off of the Internet. This folder will be under (C:) with other folders like your Documents folder. To access and unzip a new theme that you have downloaded, you will have to find it in this folder first.

This next part is for future reference if and when you do download desktop themes and need to put the new file into the appropriate folder. You can also use the steps below to move other files into different folders.

After You Have Downloaded

When I started downloading desktop themes off of the Internet and then unzipped them, I found with some of them that I couldn't find them in the Desktop Themes folder. I searched everywhere! I had unzipped them into the wrong place because I hadn't read the directions carefully! I realized then, that I had to put them into my Themes folder myself. Don't make the same mistakes that I did. Be sure to read all of the information that you can about installation, so that you aren't searching for the files after downloading and unzipping them. Thememakers vary in how they set up the installation process for their themes.

Websites that you find these themes at should have information at their websites about installation. Make sure that you try to find this information before downloading or you can refer back to the website after you have downloaded the theme. It's also very important to read the Readme.txt or Help manual that should be in the folder with the theme that you downloaded and unzipped. If you have any questions about desktop themes that you are going to download, there are several good websites to visit. These are Theme Doctor at themedoctor.com and Tucows at tucows.com. You can usually find answers to any questions that you might have about downloading and installation.

The following information is for future reference. These are directions on how to move files/folders into other folders using Windows Explorer. I've given the example of moving a new theme folder from the Unzipped folder to the Plus! Themes folder (I've had to do this several times, when I unzipped the theme into the wrong folder.) You won't need to move downloaded theme folders like I did, if you follow the directions by the thememaker for downloading and installation.

You can apply these directions, though, to any file/folder that you need to move to another folder. If you do want to use the following directions to move or copy and move a file into another folder, just substitute the file name that you need to move and folder name that you need to move the file into, with the file/folder names I've given below.

Okay, let's say that you did what I did and you unzipped a new desktop theme into your unzipped folder. To put it into your Desktop Themes Plus! folder...

-Click the Start button in the lower left-hand corner of your screen. Move your pointer up to Programs, and then across to the menu. Find Windows Explorer on the menu and click once on it to open this window.

-This window should be divided into two parts (a smaller window on the left and a larger one on the right.) If the Windows Explorer window isn't divided into two windows, find and click once on the View button on the top toolbar. Move your pointer down to Explorer Bar and then across to the small menu. Find and click once on Folders. This will put a check next to it and your window will now be divided into two parts.

-On the left side, you'll see a smaller window that is titled Folders with a list of titles like Desktop, Computer, etc. Right before some of these titles you'll see a little box with either a + sign or a – sign. Put your pointer directly over (C:) in the list and click once. You'll notice that it is now highlighted and you can see the folders in (C:) in the right window.

-Now, put your pointer directly over the little box right before (C:) that has the + sign. Click once on this small box. Watch what happens below it. All of the folders are now listed directly below it, also. And, the little box now has a – sign in it.

-Now, click once on the little box again. The list below (C:) disappears. You're probably wondering why we are doing all of this, right? Be patient, I'm going to show you an easy way to move files into another folder.

-Click once again in the box before (C:) with the + sign to show the
list. Scroll down to find the folder titled Unzipped. Put your pointer
directly over the word Unzipped and click once on it. You'll now see the
files listed in this folder, if you've unzipped any and put them in this
folder, in the larger right window.

-Next, scroll up and find the folder that is titled Program Files. Place
your pointer directly over the little box with the + sign and click once
on it.

-Now, scroll down and find the folder titled Plus! Place your pointer
directly over the little box before it with the + sign and click once on it.
Underneath it you'll see the folders Systems and Themes. The Themes
folder will have the box before it with the + sign. Click once on the little
box. You should now see the list of themes directly below it.

-Here comes the fun part. Look to the larger right window and locate
the new desktop theme folder that is in the unzipped folder. Place you
pointer directly over it and and click once on it. Then, left click if you
are right-handed or right click if you are left-handed and hold the
mouse button down.

-Next, slowly move your pointer, while holding the mouse button
down, and position it directly over the word Themes. Now, release the
mouse button. As you moved the pointer, you probably saw a black circle with a black line through it light up for a moment. Also, as you were
moving the file, you probably saw what looked like a shadow of the file
under the pointer. This is what happens when you are dragging a file.
Your new desktop theme is now in the Themes folder. Find and click
once on the Close button in the upper right-hand corner to close the
Windows Explorer window.

-If you need to copy a file/ folder into another folder, hold the Ctrl
key on your keyboard down first before clicking and holding your
mouse button and moving the file. When you begin moving the file
you'll see a little plus + sign next to the shadow image. After you've
released the mouse button, the file/ folder will be in both places.

Anytime you need to find a file or move a file into a different folder, using Windows Explorer is a good way to do it. You can follow the sample directions that I have listed above and apply them to any file that you are trying to move into a new folder. First, find the file that you need to move or copy and move in the larger white window on the right. Then locate the folder you need to move it into in the smaller white window on the left. Then drag the file to the new folder. All of this can be a little confusing at first, I know. You'll get better and faster, though, the more you practice. And, you'll start to understand what an amazing machine your computer is.

*   *   *   *   *   *

Well, I hope you enjoyed our jaunt into the Desktop Theme world. Now you have some more ways to play and have fun on your computer. If you haven't done much surfing or searching on the Internet, finding sites for themes, screen savers, and wallpapers will give you an opportunity to practice. If you are inexperienced at surfing on the Internet, I would suggest that you read the chapter, Internet Basics, before you start surfing. And now onto Email Magic!

5

Email Magic

Are you tired of emails that are always in the same black font? They become tiresome after awhile don't they? Would you like to jazz them up? How about sending an email that is funny and that you know will surely make the recipient smile? They say that a picture is worth a thousand words. They're right! Putting a beautiful image or using interesting and creative designs in your email can make all the difference. Emails don't have to be boring! They can be colorful and delightful to see and read. You could become part of an Email Revolution. No more plain emails!

The world of communications has changed virtually overnight with the advent of the Internet and email. You can now visit the world and have it come to you just by clicking your mouse. With all of the creative possibilities available to you, you can not only communicate with someone on the other side of the world; you can do it with style. I love going to my Outlook Express Inbox to see what email treasures await me from my friends. I am amazed when I receive an email from someone in South Africa. But, I especially love it when someone has taken the time to creatively and visually express themselves in an email that they've sent to me. It makes me feel special. I send creative emails for the same reason. I want the person I'm sending the email to, to know that I spent time making something special just for them. There are many free egreetings websites on the Internet that you can go to and pick out a special card to send to someone. These are great and I will give you some addresses of websites that I know of at the end of this chapter. What I want to show you, now, are fun things you can do with your emails that will be one of a kind because you made them.

Some of what I will be covering in this chapter will seem to pertain only to Outlook Express 5. If you don't have Outlook that's okay, because a lot of what I will be explaining can be done in virtually any email program. As I go through each of the steps, if it's possible, I'll include ways to accomplish these steps in email programs other than Outlook Express.

Email Options

This next section will be about setting up some of the options available to you in Outlook Express and, in particular, how to set the options so that you can send Rich Text HTML emails. If you use an email program other than Outlook, check the Options, Properties, or Help section to find out how to format this option for your email. With email programs like Hotmail there will be two titles above your new message area that say Plain Text or Rich Text HTML. Check the box next to Rich Text by clicking once inside of it. When you choose this option, you'll be able to use different colored fonts, different colored backgrounds, and with some programs there should be a stationery button you can click to choose different stationery backgrounds for your email. Take some time to explore these options that allow you to choose how you want your email program set up.

Let's start with some basics in Outlook. If you haven't taken the time to select the options that you want in your email, let's do so now. If you don't have Outlook Express, reading this section would still be a good idea as you may be able to find some of the same options in your email program.

-Okay, first open up your Outlook Express program. You don't want to be online while we are doing this, so, if you are, find the File button in the upper left-hand corner and click once on it. Look towards the bottom of the menu, then find and click on Work Offline. A small window will open up that will ask you if you want to hang up the modem. Click once on the Yes button. Anytime you are in your email program and you want to take time composing or reading emails and don't want to be online, you can use this feature. This option is especially useful if you pay for hourly Internet connections. When you are ready to send your new message, click once on the Send button. Your computer will place this new email in your Outbox folder. If you want to compose more emails continue to do so. Then, when you are ready to reconnect to the Internet and send the emails that are in your Outbox folder, just click on the Send/ Receive button near the top of your Outlook Express window.

-Now, back to Outlook Express. Look across the toolbar and click once on Tools. At the bottom of the menu you will see Options. Move your pointer down and click once on it to open the Options window.

-You'll see tabs that say General, Read, Send, Compose, Signature, Spelling, Security, Connection, and Maintenance. You should take time to go through all of these areas and make choices about your options. For right now, though, we are going to concentrate on just a few.

-First, click once on the Send tab. Under the title Sending, read through the list and check the options that you want. Towards the bottom you'll see Mail Sending Format. Click once inside the white circle to the left of HTML.

-Next, find and click once on the button that is titled HTML Settings. Find Send pictures with message towards the bottom and click in the white box to the left of it to put a check in it. Then click once on the OK button. Now you will be able to send email using pictures, fonts, and color. Yeah!

-Now, find and click once on the Compose tab. At the top of the list you'll see Compose Font. Below that will be Mail:. Directly across from

Mail, find and click once on the button that says Font settings…. This will take you to the Font window. The font that you choose here will be the font that is automatically set for every new email that you begin composing. You'll always have the option of changing this font whenever you're composing a new email. So, don't worry about it being set in stone. Look through the list and make your choices about font, style, and color. When you are done, click once on the OK button. I've got mine set at Comic Sans, size 12, regular, and blue. This font is easy to read and pleasant to look at. I almost always change this font, though. I love to try new fonts all the time.

-The Signatures tab is next. I just want you to look at this feature for a moment and think about it. If you choose to use the signature line in your email you can use it for a variety of things. Would you like to send an inspiring or fun saying out for the next week or month with all of your emails? You can type it in here and it will automatically be added at the end of all your emails. Maybe you have an important announcement coming up and don't want to have to retype it every time you send out an email. This is the place to put it. Perhaps, you've just found a great website that you want to help advertise or you've just created your own website and you want everyone to know about it. The signature line is a great way to input information to go out with every email, without having to bother with typing it every time. You can change it whenever you want. Here's what mine says:

Please visit Sherwood at his website:
http:/ / www.geocities.com/ sherwood_111/

Sherwood is a teddy bear that I designed and wrote a book about years ago. I did a fun and simple website about him and wanted everyone to know about him. This is a great way to advertise if you have a new website. So think about what you'd like to include in your signature line! Note: most email programs have the signature line as an option.

-Now, find and click once on the Spelling tab. Read through the list and check the options that you want. Checking the first two will set your email up so that, before you send an email, a spell check box will automatically open up to check your spelling. I like this option. Before I changed it, I would forget to check my spelling and send my emails out with misspelled words. When you've made your choices, click once on the Apply button at the bottom. You can read through the other options at your leisure. Now, click once on the OK button at the bottom to close the Options window.

You're all set to send dazzling emails! It's wise to note that not all email programs can receive HTML email. Boo hoo! You'll just have to experiment with friends to see if they can receive the fun stuff that you send with Outlook Express. If they can't, it's okay. There are other ways to send interesting emails. If their programs aren't set up to receive it, they'll see gobbledygook HTML coding surrounding your written message. If you know that certain friends do have Outlook Express or a comparable program and can receive HTML emails, make a mental note and then dazzle them with your lovely messages.

Keyboard Shortcuts

But wait, there's one more very important thing I want to tell you about before we get started. This feature has saved me many times. You can find it in Outlook Express and Microsoft Word and use it in any program by using a certain shortcut key. If you make a mistake, you can Undo it! When I found this out, I wasn't afraid to make mistakes anymore because I knew I could change it back. If you look up at the top of the next email message we will be composing, you'll see next to Paste, a funny little half circle arrow with the word Undo below it.

Let's say that you have accidentally deleted part of your email. Click once on the little go back Undo arrow and your deleted passage will magically return. This same feature is in Microsoft Word. But what if you're working in an email program or other program and you can't find Undo on the toolbar? What if you can't find Cut, Copy, or Paste either? Here are some keyboard shortcut commands that you can use if you can't find these buttons.

To do copy, cut, paste or delete, highlight the text first and then hit these two shortcut keys on your keyboard together at the same time. It's important that you press the two keys down together, so remember this. The Ctrl or control key is below the Shift key on your keyboard.

Ctrl + c to Copy (A copy will be placed on your Clipboard until you paste it somewhere.)

Ctrl + x to Cut (This will temporarily remove the text until you paste it somewhere else.)

Hit the Delete key on your keyboard to Delete (This will completely remove the text.)

Ctrl + v to Paste (When you want to insert or paste in text that you have cut or copied, use this shortcut. Position your cursor where you want to insert the word, sentence, or image and click once. Then use the Paste shortcut.)

Ctrl + z to Undo

When you use the Delete key you can delete a whole word that has been highlighted or delete one letter at a time by placing your cursor before the letter, clicking once, and then hitting the Delete key. Wouldn't it be nice if we had a little Undo button we could click to undo mistakes in our daily lives? But then, I guess we wouldn't learn and our lives would probably be pretty boring.

Using the shortcut keys is especially useful when you're on the Internet. I use it a lot when I want to paste in my email address instead of typing it. First, I highlight my address in my address book and then use the shortcut for Copy. Then I click in the box on the website and hit the shortcut keys for Paste. In the past, there have been times when I've typed my email address in wrong. By copying and pasting, I always get it right! Sometimes, I'll find bits of information on websites that I want to remember. I highlight the text, use the shortcut for Copy, and then open up my Microsoft Word program and paste the information there.

Okay, let's get back to having fun with emails.

Selecting Stationery In Outlook

-Underneath File in the top right-hand corner of your window, you'll see New Mail with a down arrow next to it. Click once on the down arrow to view the menu.

-At the bottom find Select Stationery and click once on it to open the Select Stationery window. Look over to the far right of this window and find and click in the white box next to Show Preview. Now you'll be able to see what each stationery file looks like in the Preview box. Take a moment and click once on each stationery file listed to preview it.

-Let's practice and have some fun with Ivy. Click once on it in the list and then click once on the OK button to open up your new message. Click inside your new message area next to the ivy.

-The far left white box with the down arrow above the message area is your font menu. Click once on the down arrow. Then, scroll down, find, and click once on Lucida Calligraphy.

-The next white box and down arrow is for font size. Click once on the down arrow and choose size 36.

-Skip across to the B, I, U, and A buttons. B is for bold font, I is for italic font, U is for underlining text, and A with the down arrow is for font color. Anytime you want your font to look different you can use one or a combination of these features. For now click once on the B and U buttons. They should now look pressed in.

-Skip A for now and the next four images and then you'll see a series of lines. If you hold your pointer over each of them for a moment, you'll see the tooltips Align Left, Center, Align Right, and Justify. Click once on the Center button. It should now look pressed in.

-Now type Greetings! Greetings should be centered at the top of your page. You'll notice that the font is a green color. Each stationery file that is installed on your computer is set up with its own font and font color to go with the color scheme of the stationery. We want to make the font a darker, richer green than the green that has been used, though. If you click the down arrow next to the A, you'll see that there really isn't a very good selection of greens. Don't worry, you have more options.

-First put your cursor bar to the left of the G in Greetings. Hold the left mouse button down or right button if you're left-handed and move your cursor bar over the word Greetings. It should now be highlighted black. Look up to the top of your screen and find the Format button on the top toolbar. Click once on it and then move your pointer down and click once on Font...on the menu.

- The Font window will now open up. Look for and find Color: at the bottom of the window on the left. Below it there will be a square button with a tiny color palette on it. Click once on this button.

-This will open up the Color window with boxes just like we used when changing the color scheme/ appearance for your computer. Do you remember? Look below and find the long button bar that says Define Custom Colors and click once on it to see the expanded color spectrum. Tada! Now you can choose a beautiful green color for your font that will compliment the Ivy stationery. When you've chosen your color, click once on the OK button to close the Color window and then click the OK button again to close the Font window.

-Move your cursor bar to the end of Greetings! and click once to remove the highlighting effect. Now your font is a deep rich green.

-Hit the Enter key on your keyboard twice to move down several lines. First, click once on the Align left button and then change the font size to 14. Click once on the B and U buttons again to remove those features. Now, type a short message to friends telling them that you're trying out this new stationery.

-When you've finished typing your message, let's have some more fun. Let's change the body of the message to a lovely dark shade of purple! Put your cursor bar right before the first letter of your message. Hold the mouse button down and move the mouse over the body of the message until it is all highlighted black. Sometimes this is a hard one to master, so keep trying. Release the mouse button when it is all highlighted. Follow the steps above to change the font color to a dark purple. When you're done changing the color, click once inside the message area to remove the highlighting effect. Note: Towards the end of this chapter, you'll learn more about different ways to highlight text. Now, we're going to do something more with this new email message and…

Outlook Symbols

-Here's a fun feature if you're sending an email to someone who you know has Outlook Express. For some reason a lot of email programs can't see what we are about to do even though they have Webdings and Wingdings in their font folders. People that have Outlook Express, though, can see it. Move your cursor bar to the end of your name at the end of the email we just created and click once. Now, go up to the font list menu, click the down arrow, and find Webdings on the font list. You'll have to scroll down quite a ways, because it's waaay down at the end of the list. When you find it, click once on it.

-Now, click on the down arrow next to A for the font color list and click once on red.

-Type a capitol Y, (shift y.) Do you now see a red heart? Fun, huh! If you want to make the heart bigger, you can highlight it and then change the font size.

-Move your cursor bar to right before G in Greetings and click once. Find Wingdings (below Webdings) on the font menu list and click once on it.

-Next, click once on the U button to undo the underline. Click on the A down arrow and then click once on the purple color box. Now type { . This is to the right of P on your keyboard and you have to hold the shift key at the same time. Do you now see a purple flower? Now, put a purple flower at the end of Greetings.

-Okay, were finished with our fun email! Which of your friends have Outlook Express? Remember that they'll be able to see the Wingdings and Webdings symbols that you put in your message. If you want to send this email to other friends who won't be able to see these symbols, you can delete them before sending.

Did you enjoy the Webdings and Wingdings? You can find these different symbols and their keyboard shortcut keys in the back of the book, see Symbols and their Shortcuts. We'll be doing more fun things with them soon.

You've now learned a few of the fun things that you can do with email. Adding stationery and using interesting and colorful fonts can really add to the visual effect of your message. We only did one little email project, but the possibilities are limitless. Imagine fun and creative ways that you can make your emails sparkle with stationery, fonts, and color. You'll never have to send another plain email again! For those of you who use an email program other than Outlook Express, remember to look for the option Rich Text HTML. This will enable you to be creative and to use color with your email messages. Also, remember to look for a button titled Stationery, to view and insert stationery backgrounds for your email messages.

Some Other Creative Options In Outlook

Let's try a few more fun things. Practicing these ways to change your emails will show you the different creative options available to you.

-This will be a simple party invitation. Open up a new message by clicking on the New Mail down arrow and then clicking once on No Stationery.

-Find the Format button on the top toolbar and click once on it. Move your pointer down to Background. A new menu will open up that says Picture…, Color, and Sound…. Move your pointer to Color and then click once on Navy blue in the new menu that opens up. Your background should now be dark blue.

-Now, click once inside the message window. Go to the font drop down menu and choose Kristen. Make your text font size 36. Click once on the B and U buttons to make your font bold and underlined. Choose the font color Fuchsia and then click once on the Center button to center your text.

-Next, hit the Enter key on your keyboard twice. Type the phrase We're having a Party! Hit the Enter key once. Change your font color to White. Type the phrase Please Come!

-Then, go back up and click once on the Format button, move your pointer to Background, and this time click once on Sound…You should now see the Background Sound window. Click once on the Browse button.

-Another Background Sound File window will open. You'll see a list of different sound files; probably wav files. We want to look at the MIDI files. Look at the bottom of the window and find Files of type:. There will be a white box with a down arrow next to it. Click the down arrow, find MIDI files and click once on it. You should now see a new list of files.

-Do you see Beethoven's 5th Symphony? If you do, click once on it and then click once on the Open button. Or you can click on another MIDI file that you recognize. We're just playing so have fun.

-You'll now be back in the other Background Sound window. Your new sound file should be in the top white box. Look under Repeat Sounds. Click in the white circle before Play the sound and then make sure that it says 1 time in the next white box. Clicking on the up and down arrows will change how many times the tune plays. Now, click once on the OK button. Waa Laa! A party invitation with music!

-To delete this email since we were just playing, click the Close button in the top right-hand corner. A small box will pop up asking if you want to save it. Click once on the No button. In the future, if you are working on something Offline and want to finish it later, just click the Close button and then click Yes, when it asks you if you want to save it. This will place it in the Drafts folder and you can work on it later.

-Maybe you've finished the email, but want to send it later. There's another way to save an email to the Drafts folder if you want to send it later. When you've finished getting it ready to send, don't click the Send button. Instead, find the File button on the far left of your top toolbar and click once on it. A menu will pop down. Move your pointer down to Save on the list and click once. A little window will open up telling you that your computer is going to put the email in your Drafts folder. Click once on the OK button. Then, it will be in your Drafts folder until you are ready to send it.

-When you are ready to send it, click once on the Drafts folder (it's below your Deleted folder.) This will open up the folder and you'll see your email in the window on the right. Double click on the email to open it up and then click once on your Send button.

Your computer was probably sent with a short list of MIDI files installed. You can also find more on the Internet for free and download them. Searching for MIDI files is just like searching for anything else.

Start with the search sites first and then begin surfing the individual websites. If you have any questions about downloading MIDI files off of a website, email the website owner. You can usually find an Email Me or Contact Me button somewhere on the website.

Inserting Pictures Into Email

The one feature that we didn't work with was inserting pictures. You may or may not have pictures on file. If you do, you can practice inserting them into an email to send to friends. You can send pictures with an email as an attachment or you can insert them directly into the email, if you have an email program like Outlook that allows you to insert them.

There are two formats of picture files that work well for insertion in Outlook emails. They are JPG or JPEG (Joint Photographic Expert Group) which is a compressed file format that works well for photos. These files are quite small and are great for use in emails. The other format is GIF (Graphics Interchange Format). GIF is best used for clip art and solid images rather than for photos. A picture in a mixed format will not insert into an email.

There are many free clip art websites where you can find interesting clip art. All you have to do is search. Always check the description first, though, if you are looking for images that you can insert in email. Make sure they are in the JPEG or GIF format. I like to find images of angels, flowers, hearts, or any image that will make someone smile.

There is one other way of obtaining pictures on the Internet that a lot of attention has been focused on lately. It is very easy to copy any image into one of your folders that you see on the Internet or on any website. Placing your mouse pointer over an image and then right clicking once (left clicking if you are left-handed) will cause a small window to open up. Midway down the menu you will see Save picture as.... If you click on this title a new window will open up that will allow you to put a copy of the image into one of your folders. As an artist, this is one issue that concerns me and many other artists and website designers who work hard to create beautiful images. This is what you will do when saving wallpaper images, also, but the concept is different because the website owners are offering their images free to the public and so it is alright to save them to your computer.

Anytime you see an image on a website that you like, always read the disclaimers or find information the website designer may have posted about the images. Many websites will tell you that it is okay to use for free what they have put on their site as long as it's not for commercial use. Others will ask you to email them for permission. Others require that you pay. Many designers have begun watermarking their images. This imprints their name, etc., on their images; much like a signature except that it cannot be removed.

I recently went to the website of a very well known artist. A beautiful image of one of his paintings was on his homepage. I thought this was interesting as his paintings are very expensive and I thought that this large image could probably be easily copied. So, I decided to see if he had any stop guards in place to prevent this. When I right clicked on the image a window came up that said, Sorry, you cannot copy this image. I thought, 'Hooray!' Someone finally figured out how to padlock images. So, if you see an image that you would like to use, be sure to read the information given on the website and respect the creativity and hard work of artists and designers.

If you want to practice inserting pictures, and you have some pictures on file in either JPEG or GIF format, here's what you do.

-Open a new message with no stationery. First, click in the white message area. It's important that you do this first or you will not be able to access your pictures. Find and click once on the Insert button on the top toolbar. Find Picture…on the menu and click once on it to open the Picture window.

-Click once on the Browse button to open the Picture file window. Make sure that it says (C:) in the white box next to Look in:. If it doesn't, you can click on the folder icon with the up arrow, tooltip Up One Level, until you see (C:) in the white box.

-Now you should be able to see all of the folders in (C:). Where are your pictures? Find the folder that they are in and double click on this folder. Now you should be able to see all of the GIF and JPEG files. When you see the one you want, click once on it and then click once on the Open button. Then click the OK button in the Picture window. Your picture should now be inserted in your email.

-Click once on the image to size it and position it. When you've done this you should see small white boxes positioned around the outside edge of the picture. When you move your cursor bar over the picture, you're cursor will change into a four-sided arrow. If you would like your picture to be centered, click once on the Center button or choose one of the other buttons to align the picture.

-If you want to make the picture a different size, first hold your cursor over one of the white boxes until it turns into a two-sided arrow ↔ ↕. If you hold the cursor over the top or bottom white box it will turn into a up/down arrow. If you hold your cursor over one of the white boxes on either side of the picture, it will turn into a side to side arrow. When you see one of these arrows, hold you mouse button down and then move your mouse to make the picture smaller or larger.

-When you have the picture the size that you want it, click in the message area to the right of the picture, hit the Enter key on your keyboard several times, and then you can begin typing. You will need to click the Align Left button if you have centered your picture and you want to type beginning on the left margin.

-If you want the picture to be at the end of your message, click once on the picture. Find the Cut button in the upper left-hand corner of your window and click once on it. This will remove your picture from sight. Don't worry though, we're going to bring it right back. Click once at the end of your message and then hit the Enter key on your keyboard once. Now find the Paste button to the right of the Cut and Copy button and click once on it. Your picture should now be at the end of your message. Click once on the picture if you want to align it.

-If you want the picture in the middle of your message or anywhere else in your message, follow these same steps except click at the end of the line of text that you want the picture to go under. Hit the Enter key once and then the Paste button once.

-Sometimes I like to have small pictures at the beginning and at the end of my message. To copy a picture, follow these same steps except click the Copy button instead of the Cut button and then Paste the image to insert it wherever you would like in the message.

With some email programs you are not able to insert pictures, but you can send pictures as an attachment. So, keep this in mind when sending emails. It's always good to keep in mind, also, that graphics are larger files than just plain text. When you insert a graphic or picture in your email or send them as an attachment, your email file will be larger than an email that has just text in it. JPEG and GIF formats are great because they keep the graphics file small, but they will still be larger than a plain text email. I don't mind, though, because I love receiving and sending creative and colorful emails. To me it's worth waiting for an email to download when I know that I will be delighted when I open it up.

Have you ever received a video attachment in an email? If you have, you know that a video is a very large graphics file because it takes a very long time to download. If you ever want to send a video attachment to friends, choose a time when the Internet isn't busy. I go over information about peak Internet times in the chapter, Internet Basics.

If you are able to insert pictures into your email, remember that the person you are sending the email to might not receive it the way you've sent it. Some email programs will convert an inserted image into a separate download. The person receiving it will have to download the picture in a separate window. Oh well...at least they will still get the picture, right?

What if someone sends you an email with a picture inserted and you love the picture so much, that you would like to save it to one of your folders so that you can use it later. How do you do this? Find out next...

-Place your pointer over the picture and right click your mouse. A small menu will pop up.

-Move your pointer to and click once on Save Picture As....

-The Save Picture window will open up.

-At the top you'll see Save in: with a white box next to it. It might say Pictures in this white box. If it says My Documents, look down into the large white box that has the files and folders listed. Find the folder that has Pictures next to it and double click on it. This will open up the Pictures folder where you are saving all of your pictures (or you may have another folder that you are saving your pictures to.)

-Find File name: and the white box next to it near the bottom of the Save Picture window. You can put a new name for the picture you are saving in this white box if you want to. If the name in it is highlighted, you can hit the Delete key on your keyboard to clear it. Or, you can click inside the white box and hit your Delete key or your Backspace key to clear it.

-Type the name you have chosen for your picture in this white box.

-Click once on the Save button to save it in the folder that you've chosen to keep it in.

Wonderful WordArt Attachments

What if you don't have an email program that allows you to do a lot of this fun stuff? Don't despair! You can still be creative and have fun. We are going to make a beautiful WordArt document to send via email as an attachment. These attachments can be used with any email program.

For our next email project you need to open up a new document in Microsoft Word. Click once on the Start button, move your pointer up to Programs and then across to the next menu. When you find Microsoft Word click once on it and this will open up a new document. We are going to check first to see what toolbars you have available and then set your document options to my preferences. You can always change them and customize them later if you want to.

-First click once on the View button on the top toolbar to see the drop down menu. Move your pointer down and find Page Layout. You'll see a button to the left of it when you highlight it. Is the button pressed in? If it isn't, you aren't in the Page Layout view. I think this is the easiest one to work in, so click once on Page Layout if the button isn't pressed in.

-Go back and click on the View button again and move your pointer down to Toolbars. A new menu will open up. Look on the list to see if these titles have a check to the left of them: Standard, Formatting, Drawing, Forms, Picture, Tables and Borders. If you don't see a check next to them, take a moment and click on each one of them to add these toolbars to your Word screen. Under Toolbars on the View menu make sure that Ruler has a check next to it, also. If it doesn't, click once on Ruler to check it.

-Now, find and click once on the Tools button on the top toolbar. Move your pointer down to Options…and click once on it to open that window. Next, click once on the General tab. Towards the bottom you'll see Mail as attachment with a white box before it. Make sure that there is a check in this box. This will allow you to send Word documents as attachments. I would also suggest that you take some time later and read through all of the options available to you under each tab title so that you can select what further options you might want for Microsoft Word.

-Next, look up to the right of your Word window and find the small white box that has a down arrow next to it and a number with a % sign next to it. The tooltip is Zoom. Click the down arrow, find 75% and click once on it. I find that this is the easiest window to work in when I am making a WordArt attachment.

-Now, this is just a project to help you imagine the creative possibilities available to you with Word. Let's say that you have a friend who is feeling down and you want to send a note to let them know you are thinking of them. Let's put a border on the page first. Click once on the Format button on the top toolbar and when you see Borders and Shading…on the menu, click once on it to open the Borders and Shading window.

-Click once on the Page Border tab. Under Setting, click on the large white button with a document in it next to Box.

-In the middle column you'll see Style, Color, Width, and Art. Click on the down arrow below Style to view your border choices. Scroll down the list and when you see the border style that looks like a rope, click once on it.

-Next, look down to Color: and click the down arrow to view the color choices. When you see red, click once on it to put it in the Color: box.

-Look down to Width: and you'll see that it says 3 pt. This is the only width choice for this particular border. Later, when you have some time, click the down arrow under Art: to view the neat choices that you have available for borders. There are some really great ones. For now we are going to be using the rope border for our project.

-Now, look over to the Preview window. Below it you'll see Apply to. It should say Whole Document in the white box. If it doesn't, click the down arrow, find it on the list, and click once on it to put it in the box. Click once on the OK button to return to your document. You should now see a red rope border. Neat!

- Let's stop for a moment and save this document to a folder. Click once on the File button on the top toolbar. Find and click once on Save As…on the menu to open the Save As window. In the white box next to Save in: at the top of the new window, you'll probably see the folder My Documents. You can put it in another folder if you want to, but this folder will probably already have a shortcut icon on your Desktop and is easy to access. I use this folder a lot.

-Towards the bottom of the window you'll see File name:. It will probably say something like Doc 1 and will be highlighted. If the file name is highlighted, hit the Delete key on your keyboard to clear it. If the file name isn't highlighted, click once inside the white box and then hit the Delete key or the Backspace key to delete it. Then, type in a name for your new file that will help you remember it. Click once on the Save button in the upper right-hand corner.

Note: Always save, save, save! When you're working on a project or document, be sure to save it often. I had been told this and thought I was pretty good at doing it. When I was writing one of the chapters for this book, I wanted to check something out in another chapter. I looked in the other chapter, came back to what I was writing and most of it was gone! I'd forgotten to save it before taking a shortcut to the other chapter. If you haven't saved the document in a folder, i.e. Save As…, do that first. After that, when you save changes to a document that you've already saved in a folder, all you have to do is click the File button on your top toolbar and then click once on Save.

When you close a document window by clicking the Close button in the top right-hand corner and you haven't saved the changes, your computer will ask you if you want to save the changes you've just made. Always click the Yes button. When I am working on a new project, I click on Save at about five minute intervals. If there are power surges that shut down your computer or your program goofs up for some reason, you won't lose material that you've saved.

You can also set up how often your computer automatically saves your changes for you. To do this, find and click once on the Tools button on the top toolbar. Move your pointer down and click once on Options…to open up this window. Click on the Save tab and select the options that you want and how often you want the Save Auto recovery set. Also, be sure to read the information at the end of Chapter 6, Let's

Play Some More, about copying and saving important information onto floppy discs.

-Now let's do a colorful three-dimensional note. Look below your document and find the toolbar that says Draw and Autoshapes.

-Find and click once on Autoshapes. A new menu will open up that has the titles Lines, Basic Shapes, Block Arrows, Flowchart, Stars and Banners, and Callouts. Hold your pointer over each of these titles for a moment to see the menus of each one.

-Now, go back to Basic Shapes and find and click on the heart shape in the menu. Notice how your pointer changes into a + when you move it to an area on your document page. When you see this symbol, click your mouse button once. Presto, there's a heart! The heart will be white inside and you will see small white boxes on each side of it that will allow you to make the heart any size that you want. For now, just leave it the size it is because we are going to change the inside color and border color first.

-Across from AutoShapes on the bottom toolbar you'll see a little paint can, a little paint brush tip, an A, lines, arrows, a box with shading and a three dimensional box. Hold your pointer over each one of these for a moment to read the tooltip for each one. These are the options that you can use for AutoShapes and the Text Box. We'll be using some of these options for the heart you just put in your message.

-Click on the tiny down arrow next to the paint can to open up the color menu window. The color you choose in this window will fill the heart with color. Look to the bottom of this little window and find and click once on Fill Effects…. This will open up the Fill Effects window. You'll see tabs that say Gradient, Texture, Pattern, and Picture. When you have time, take a moment to check each of these tabs out and play with all of the options. There are some amazing ones that you can use to fill objects with color! For now, click once on the Gradient tab.

-We are going to fill our heart with two colors. So, under Colors click in the white circle to the left of Two colors. Now you'll see to the right

Color 1: and below that Color 2:. Leave the Color 1 white. If it isn't already at white, click the down arrow and choose white.

-Next, click the down arrow under Color 2:. Click once on More Colors…at the bottom of the menu. You'll see a new window open up called Colors with two tabs titled Standard and Custom. Make sure that you are in the Standard tab window. If you aren't, click once on this tab. You'll see a color chart with many different colors. Find a dark red colored hexagon and click once on it. Now, click once on the OK button. Note: If you were working on a project, and couldn't find the color you wanted in this color chart, you could click on the Custom tab to customize your color.

-Under Colors, you'll see Shading styles:. Take a moment to click in the white circle to the left of each title, Horizontal, Vertical, Diagonal up, Diagonal down, From corner, and From center. Watch to the right, under the Variants title, to see the Variants preview boxes and also watch the Sample preview box in the lower right-hand corner. These will show you how the different shading styles will look.

-For now we are going to use the From Center shading style, so click in the white circle next to it. Look under the Variants title to view the boxes. One will have the white color in the center and the other one will have the red color in the center. Take a moment and click one each of these boxes and watch the Sample box. This feature allows you to change the order of the colors. Click back on the Variant box that shows the white color in the middle. Then click once on the OK button to return to your document. Wow, a lovely red heart with a white center!

-We now want to change the line border to the same color as the heart. Find the little paintbrush tip next to the paint can and click on the down arrow. You will see the color menu again with color boxes. Below these boxes you will see one colored box with the red that you chose for your heart. Click once on this red box. This is a great color feature because it saves you the trouble of clicking on, More colors, and finding the color you used before in the Colors window. You don't have to use the same red color if you don't want to. The line border can be any color and any line style that you want it to be. For our project, though, we are going to leave it the same red color.

-Next to A, on the bottom toolbar, you'll see three lines. When you hold your pointer over them, the tooltip will say Line Style. Click once on the lines and the menu will show you the different line thickness' that you can use for the outside line border. For now we are going to use ¾ pt. Make sure that it is pressed in on the menu, by clicking once on it.

-Our heart is finished! We will resize it in a little bit.

-To the right of Autoshapes on the bottom toolbar you'll see a line, an arrow, a rectangle, and an oval. Put your pointer over the next shape and you'll see the tooltip that says Text box and then the next one, a floating A, will be Insert WordArt. Click once on the floating A to open up the WordArt Gallery window. You'll see boxes with different styles and colors that you can use for your WordArt. Click once on the box that is in the very top left-hand corner and then click once on the OK button.

-A new window will open up that is called Edit WordArt Text. First hit the Delete key on your keyboard to remove the words Your Text Here. Now, choose the font Monotype Corsiva from the font menu, font size 20 from the size menu, and click the B button for bold.

-Click once inside the message area and type Thinking of You…and then click once on the OK button. There's your message, looking white and empty on the page. Don't worry, though, we're going to do some neat stuff to it! A little WordArt window will now be on your screen, also.

-Click once on the little paint can in this small WordArt window. This new window will be Format WordArt. You'll see the tabs Colors and Lines, Size, Position, and Wrapping. Take a moment to click on and view each tab. Click back to the tab titled Colors and Lines.

-Under Fill, click the down arrow next to the Color: box. Find and click once on Fill Effects…at the bottom of the menu. Now we're back in the Fill Effects window that we used to fill the heart. Let's try a Preset option! Click in the white circle next to Preset. To the right of this you'll see Preset colors:. Click the down arrow below this title. Scroll down, find, and then click once on Early Sunset.

-Under Shading styles, click in the white box to the left of Horizontal.

-Under Variants there should now be four viewing boxes. Find and click once on the box that has the orange/ red color running through the center. It should be in the lower left-hand corner. Click once on the OK button to return to the Format WordArt window.

-Under Line: you'll see Color:, Dashed:, and Weight:. In the white box next to Color:, click the down arrow and find and click on a dark purple color. In the white box next to Dashed:, click the down arrow and find and click on the solid line. In the white box next to Weight:, click either the down or up arrow to select 1.5 pt.

-Click once on the OK button to return to your document. What do you think? Isn't your phrase, Thinking of you…, lovely? Let's make sure that the phrase is centered. In the small WordArt window look for the Center lines that we've used before. They are on the bottom row. If you hold your pointer over the lines, you'll see the tooltip WordArt Alignment. Click on the lines and make sure the lines to the left of Center are pressed in.

-Now, let's do another WordArt phrase. Start by clicking once on the floating A on the bottom toolbar. Follow the same steps as you did when you made the WordArt phrase, Thinking of You…. There will be one difference, though. When you click in the Text: area of the Edit WordArt Text window make sure that you hit the Enter key on your keyboard before you type the second line of your phrase.

-Type the phrase, And Sending You Thoughts of (hit the Enter key and then type the second line) Sunshine and Good Things!. If you don't hit the Enter key, the phrase will be typed in one continuous line that will extend off of the page and it will be difficult to resize and change. Fill this phrase with the same Preset, Early Sunset, and the same line color and weight as the first phrase by following the previous steps.

-Now, let's move the heart to the center of your document. Move your pointer over the heart, until you see the four-sided arrow. Click your mouse button once. The little white boxes are back and you're ready to move the heart. Click and hold the mouse button and move your pointer to the center of your document. The heart will move also. Release the mouse button.

-Now, do the same thing with the WordArt phrases Thinking of you…and Sending You Thoughts of Sunshine and Good Things!. Move Thinking of You…to the top of your document. Move Sending You Thoughts…to the bottom of your document. Resize the phrases so that they are approximately a ½ inch from the red rope border on three sides and so that the letters are approximately 2 inches tall in the first phrase and 1 inch tall in the second phrase. Do this by moving your cursor over the white boxes until you see the two-sided arrow. Click, hold, and move your mouse to resize the phrases.

-How about changing the shape of your phrases? Straight is okay, but curved is even better! Click once on the first phrase, Thinking of You…. Find and click once on the letters Abc, next to the little paint can, in the small WordArt window. The tooltip for Abc is WordArt Shape. This new window will display different shapes. You can click on any of these to alter the shape of your WordArt in fun ways. We're going to use the one called Can Up for the first phrase. Find the shape that is in the third row down and third from the left. Hold your pointer over it for a moment to see the tooltip. It should say, Can Up. Click once on this shape. Does your first phrase now have a nice downward curve to it?

-Now, click on the second phrase And Sending You…. Change the shape of this phrase to Can Down. You will find it right next to Can Up in the WordArt shape window. It should now have a nice upward curve to it. Remember to take some time later to play with all of these different shapes for WordArt.

-Let's resize and center the heart now. Move it so that is centered in the middle of the document. Now, resize it. You can make it large, medium, or small. It's up to you.

-This next step will add dimension and fullness to your creation! Click on the WordArt phrase, Thinking of You.... Now look to the right of the paintbrush, A, lines and arrows on the bottom toolbar. You should see a square with a shadow. The tooltip for it is Shadow. Click once on the Shadow button to open up the Shadow window.

-There will be rows of different styles of shadowed squares. Find the square that has a shadow that shows to the bottom right of it. It should be in the fourth row down and second from the left. The tooltip for this square is Shadow Style 14. Click once on Shadow Style 14. Your first phrase will now have a subtle gray shadow to it that will make it stand out attractively from the page. Do you like the gray color of the shadow? I don't. I want every aspect of my WordArt to be colorful. Don't you? Great! So let's change it to a blue shadow. Here's how.

-Click again on the Shadow box on the bottom toolbar. At the bottom of the window find and click on Shadow Settings.... This will open up a small Shadow Settings window.

-Find the square with a shadow on the far right that has a down arrow to the right of it. Click on the down arrow. There are those great color boxes again! But we want more of a selection, so click on More Shadow Colors...at the bottom of this new window. The Colors window will open up with the tabs Standard and Custom. Click once on the Standard tab to find a subtle blue color to use as your shadow color. If you can't find a color that you like, click on one that is close and then click on the Custom tab to adjust it. When you've found your color, click once on the OK button to close this window. Look at your phrase. What do you think? Do you like the new blue shadow? Play some more if you need to. When you've made your final choice, click on the Close button in the Shadow Settings window to close it.

-Now, click on the second phrase And Sending You…. Follow the previous steps to add a lovely subtle blue shadow to the second phrase. Remember to look at the row directly below all of the colored boxes to find the blue color that you just used for the shadow in the first phrase. This great feature makes it so much easier to find the color you just used, especially if it's a customized color.

-Next, we are going to add the same shadow to the heart but with a bit of a difference. First, follow the previous steps and give your heart the same blue shadow. Now, click again on the down arrow in the small Shadow Settings window. Find and click on Semitransparent Shadow in this new window. This feature lightens up the shadow on an object and makes it stand out even more. We're finished! What do you think? Wouldn't you love to receive this simple loving message if you were feeling down? Let's get it ready to be emailed.

-We've worked on this document in the 75% zoom window. Change the zoom to 50%. When you're friend receives this via email which size would you like her or him to read it in? 50% or 75%? Make your choice.

-Now, let's save the final changes that you've made. Click once on the File button on the top toolbar and then find and click once on Save on the menu.

-We're ready to email! If you're using an email program like Outlook Express that you have installed on your computer, click once on File on the top toolbar and move your pointer down to Send To…. Slide your pointer over to Mail Recipient…and click once.

-Click in the email message area and type this message or something similar…Hi! I'm sending you an attachment that I made in my Word program. The attachment is perfectly safe to open. If you're worried, email me and I'll confirm that it is okay.

-Put in your friend's address, type a subject in the Subject: box, and click Send! With all of the media coverage about email attachment viruses, it's always a good idea to send this type of message with any attachment that you send.

-If you are using an email program like Hotmail, Yahoo, AOL, etc., first close this new word document. Then connect to your email account, compose your new email message about the attachment being okay to open and then find and click once on the Attachment or Attach button. Read the directions in this new window. Then, click the browse button to find the folder that you saved this file/ document in and double click on it. Now, find the file name that you saved the document under. Click once on the file name to highlight it and then click the OK button.

-This will put the file in the attachment window in your email program. Follow the directions given and then send your email.

The email WordArt document that we just created to send as an attachment could have also been printed out and given to a friend or mailed to a friend that doesn't have a computer. Do you have a color printer? If you don't, do you have a friend who does? Some of my friends don't have printers. So, when they need something printed out they just email it to me and I print it out for them. If this was a project that you decided you wanted to print and you have a friend who would print it for you, you could have emailed the document as an attachment to your friend. What if you don't know anyone who has a printer? Do you have a store near you that provides copying services for the public? Give them a call and see if you can either email them the document or bring it in on a floppy disc for them to copy for you. You don't have to limit yourself creatively if you don't have a printer.

What if you have a printer, but it isn't a color printer? You can make your WordArt and AutoShapes shaded with the same options we used in the Fill Effects window. Just choose the One color option to shade the fill area, or don't fill the space with anything and experiment with interesting line borders. Then print the document on some of the neat colored printing paper that is available. Remember the sky is the limit and you are not bound creatively!

You're learning valuable creative and technical skills that will help you when you work in any program that you use on your computer.

The process, at first, may seem to take a long time. Everything does in the beginning, when you're learning. As you play, have fun, and experiment, you'll be practicing and you'll get faster. Soon, you'll be zip clicking and making colorful and artistic creations quickly and easily!

Microsoft Graphics Studio Greetings 99 and Clip Art

When I bought my computer, it came with Windows 98 2nd Edition. One of the CD's that came with this package was called Microsoft Graphics Studio Greetings 99. I know other people who received the same CD and have never taken the time to see what's on it. Do you have this CD? If you do, have you taken some time to review it? If you haven't, check it out! I have made so many wonderful cards with this program and the clip art files on it are amazing! Plus you can send anything you make in it, whether it is a card or flyer, via email. There's even a special email section that shows you how to do animation and sounds with the email that you send. So, if you haven't taken the time to experiment and play with this CD, please do.

Even if you don't make anything with it, you can use the clip art file available on the CD to really enhance your other fun projects by inserting wonderful and colorful images. If you want to just see what's included in the Microsoft Clip Gallery 5.0, you can find it by clicking the Start button on your bottom taskbar, moving up to Programs, and then finding and clicking on it in the Programs menu. This will open up the Microsoft Clip Gallery window. You can click on each of the categories to view the contents or you can type a key word in the top search box and then hit your Enter key. For instance, if you want to see what kind of angel clips there are, type angel in the search box and hit the Enter key on your keyboard. It will search for and group all of the angel pictures for you to see. If you want to go back to the category list, just click the left pointing arrow in the top left-hand corner. If you don't understand what some of the features are, just hold your pointer over them to see the tooltip.

You won't be able to use any of the clip art, though, unless you have the Greetings CD in your CD-ROM. The clip art file on this CD can be installed on your hard drive so that you don't have to insert the CD every time you want to use clips. It's a large file, though, and will take up a lot of space on your hard drive if you choose to install it. I've chosen not to do this because I want to conserve the space that I have on my hard drive. So, whenever I'm ready to be creative, I just pop the CD in and start inserting clips!

There is also a small file of images installed on your computer for your use in documents. Let's take a moment to just check these out.

-Open a new document by clicking the Start button, moving your cursor up to Programs, and then finding and clicking once on Microsoft Word. Find and click once on the Insert button on the top toolbar. Move your pointer down to Picture. Find and click once on From File…in the next small menu. (You can also access the clip art on the Greetings CD, if you have it, from here by clicking on Clip Art….) A new window titled Insert Picture will open up and you will see a list of folders titled Backgrounds, Bullets, Lines, and Popular.

-Double click on the Popular folder. Take a moment to click once on and preview each image on the list. To insert any of these images into a document, just click on the Insert button in the upper right-hand corner.

-To view another folder and its contents, click on the yellow folder that has the up arrow next to the Look in: box. The tooltip for this yellow folder is Up One Level and it will return you to the window where you can view the other folders.

-You can also insert a picture from one of your folders this way. Click the Up One Level folder until you see (C:) in the white box with the down arrow next to it. Find the folder that your pictures are in and double click on it to view your pictures. Click once on the Insert button to insert the picture that you've chosen.

-To return to the Popular, Backgrounds, Bullets, and Lines folders, go back to (C:), by clicking on the Up One Level folder. Then find and double click on Program Files.

-Next, find and double click on the folder Microsoft Office. Double click on the Clip art folder and you'll be back to the original window.

-Make sure the white box to the left of Float over Text on the right side of the Insert Picture window is checked if you use a clip or picture in your document. This will make it easy to resize and move your image.

-If you insert any images from the Clip Gallery 5.0 CD or the installed clip art files, just click on them as you did the WordArt and AutoShape images to resize and move them.

Symbol Email Attachments

We are now going to really play! This next project is one that I like to do when I want to send something to a friend via email that I know will make them laugh and smile. If they can't view symbols in their regular email program, they will be able to view them in a word document attachment. We're going to learn how to make a Symbol email attachment. You can also use any of these symbols in documents to emphasize a point. Or, you can use them in a flyer, a card, or a fun document project. Use your imagination and don't be afraid to get goofy. To see a sample of a symbol email that I did once, look in the back of this book for Silly Symbol Email Attachment. I composed this symbol email after a friend had called earlier in the evening needing my help because she was having a problem with her computer. I decided some humor was in order, so I sent her this email.

-Open up a new document. We are first going to learn how to access these symbols in your Word program, view them, and insert them.

There is also a list of common symbols with their corresponding keyboard shortcuts in the back of this book that you can use for reference if you're working on a project. To use the keyboard shortcuts, remember to use the font menu to find the font first as we did when we used them in the email message earlier.

-Find and click once on the Insert button on the top toolbar. Move your pointer down and find and click once on Symbol…in the menu to open up the Symbol window. You'll see two tabs titled Symbols and Special Characters. Make sure you are in the tab window titled Symbols.

-Find Font: and the white box next to it and then click the down arrow. This is a menu of the different fonts that have symbols in them. Scroll down the list and find and click once on Webdings.

-You'll see lots of little boxes with lots of little symbols that are so small it's hard to tell what some of them are. To see a bigger picture of a symbol, pick a box and click once on it. A larger box will appear with a larger image. Practice clicking on some of the boxes.

-Pick out a symbol to use and click on the box that it is in. Find and click once on the Insert button in the lower right-hand corner of the window. Then, click once on the Close button.

-You'll see that it is now on your new document page. It's so tiny, though. To make it bigger, highlight it and then choose a larger font size from the font size menu.

-Next, choose a color for it by clicking on the down arrow right after A, which is on the toolbar right above your document area. Click once inside the document area to remove the highlighting effect. What do you think? Pretty nifty, huh?

-Next, type the sentence, We are going to put our on the market. Go back to the Symbol window, by clicking on the Insert button and then Symbol. Find the house symbol in Webdings. When you've found it, click once on it and then click once on the Insert button and then the Close button.

-Highlight the house symbol and then choose the font size 22 and the font color dark red. Next, click once on the Cut button. In Microsoft Word the Cut button looks like a pair of scissors on the toolbar near the upper left-hand corner.

-Put your cursor right after the, r, in the word, our, of your sentence and click once. Now, click once on the Paste button. It's across from the Cut button and looks like a clipboard on your toolbar. You should now see the house in the middle of your sentence.

-Anytime you want to insert a symbol, you can also place your cursor in the sentence where you want the symbol to go and click once. Then, click once on the Insert button and then the Symbol button. Select your symbol and then click once on Insert and then Close. This will place the symbol right where you need it and you won't have to cut and paste it.

-Take some time and check out the other symbol fonts in the Symbol window. There are some really interesting symbols that you can use. Experiment and make up your own silly symbol email attachment.

I've been known to be pretty corny. I think corny is good. When I sent the symbol email that you saw in the back of the book to my friend as an attachment, she loved it. She told people about it and suggested that I send it to them just so they could have a good laugh, too. I did. I like to make people smile and laugh and help them to lighten up when life is hard. Don't you? Think about how you could send a fun symbol email attachment to someone you know. Don't be afraid to be really corny. It will make their day.

Forwarded Follies

Let's take a moment to cover an important email option that we haven't talked about yet. Have you ever received a forwarded email that has a lot of addresses, including yours in the message header? Then you look down to the message itself and you see lots of email addresses that you have to scroll down through in order to find the message? We'll learn how to clean up these addresses in the message in a minute, but first let's talk about hiding those addresses in the message header.

Let's say that you have an email message that you want to send out to lots of people. When you're ready to input all of the addresses, you should see the address bars at the top of your message window that say To: and Cc:. But do you see Bcc:? Do you know what Bcc: is for? Internet etiquette or what they call netiquette suggests that if you are sending out an email to many people, it isn't polite to show all of the email addresses. That's what Bcc: is for. You can type the addresses next to Bcc: in the address box and they won't be shown. The only thing that people will see when they've received the email is that the email has been sent to Undisclosed recipients. This keeps your friend's addresses private and prevents the possibility of them being compiled and put on emailing lists. Note: Another netiquette suggestion is that you always type your messages in the lower case, except when you need to capitalize a new word, etc. TYPING WORDS WITH ALL CAPS IS CONSIDERED SHOUTING. So, unless you really do mean to be shouting at someone (which I hope you aren't doing) type your messages normally.

Bcc: is an important feature and should be used if possible. I don't worry about my friends seeing my private email address because they all know me and I trust them. But, I am concerned about emails that continue to be forwarded on and on into infinity, as some undoubtedly are, to many people that I don't know. Someone along the way, who doesn't know me, may collect email addresses for an emailing list. There is nothing worse that getting unsolicited advertisements or nasty emails in your mailbox. It's tedious and aggravating to have to delete and block emails that you don't want to receive. You can prevent your friend's email addresses from being accessed by people they don't know by following these next steps. If you don't see Bcc: under To: and Cc: in your message header, here's how to access it.

-If you have Outlook Express as your email program, open up a new message. Find and click once on the View button on the top toolbar. When the menu comes down, the first item will be All Headers. Click once on All Headers and a check mark will now appear next to it. You'll now see Bcc: below Cc: and To:. When you want to send out a message to lots of people, use the Bcc: address box instead of To:, to hide your friend's addresses. When they all receive the email, all they will see is that the email has been sent to Undisclosed recipients. Then, if they choose to forward the email on and their friends forward it on and their friends forward it on…your friend's addresses will never be seen.

-Some email programs like AOL don't have this address field. But, if you put parentheses around each email address, they will be sent out hidden just as if your were using the Bcc: address box.

-What if you use Hotmail, Yahoo, or another email program? When you're composing a new message, check to see if you have all three address boxes, i.e. To:, Cc:, and Bcc:, in your new message header. If you don't see all three address boxes, and you're not sure how to do this in your email program find and click on View, Options, Properties, or find the Help section for your email program to find answers on how to hide addresses. Your friends will thank you and you can encourage them to follow these same steps so that your address is always hidden.

Now we're going to learn how to clean up forwarded emails that you want to forward on to your friends. This is serious business. So pay close attention as we whisk away unwanted email clutter! We're going to learn how to forward without also sending addresses from all the other Forwards. And…we're going to learn how to forward a Forward without sending all those Forwards that you sometimes have to click through when you get a Forward! You can clean up emails in any email program.

Here's the scenario…You've gotten an email that says Fw:Fw:Fw:Fw:…in the message line and it has the paperclip attachment symbol next to it. You double click on it to open up the forwarded message and all you see is a blank page. So, you double click on the Fw: in the attachment box to open up what you think will be the message and you see another blank page. You double click the Fw: again and the next window has some addresses and parts of messages, but nothing worth reading!! Now, you're getting impatient. So, you double click on the Fw: in the attachment box again thinking, 'If this isn't the message I'm supposed to be receiving, I'm going to delete, with gleeful abandon, this whole email!' In this next message window, you scroll through lists of email addresses of people you don't know and fiiinnnaaallly, down at the bottom, you see the message! Frustrating, isn't it? Would you like to learn how Not to do this if you decide that you want to send the message on to your friends? You would? Great! Let's get started.

-After reading the message and deciding you would like to send it on to others, stay put. Don't go back to your Inbox and forward from there. Stay in the window that you are reading the message in. We are going to send a brand new, clean email message.

-Do you remember the keyboard shortcut keys for Copy and Paste? Do you remember how to highlight a section of text? We are going to be doing this again. Put your cursor in front of the first letter of the text section you want to send on to your friends (don't highlight the addresses.) Click your mouse button and hold it while you move your mouse over this section of text. Release your mouse button. The message you want to send on will now be highlighted.

-Now, hold down the two keys on your keyboard, Ctrl + c at the same time, for a second to copy this text. The text has now been copied onto your Clipboard. You can't see it, but it's there, so don't worry.

-If your email program is Outlook, find and click once on the File button on the far left of the top toolbar of your message window. When the menu comes down you'll see that the first title is New with a right pointing arrow next to it. Slide your mouse over to the arrow and a new menu will open up. Click once on Mail message. This will open up a new mail message window for you.

-If you are using an email program other than Outlook, find the Compose, Write, or New Mail button and click on it to open up your new message window. Note: Remember that this is a new message, not a forward or reply.

-Now, click once inside the new message area. It's important that you do this first.

-Next, hold down the two keys on your keyboard, Ctrl + v at the same time, for a second, to paste in the text that you just copied. Your copied text will now be pasted into your new message. Since you copied only the message you wanted to send on (and not all of those addresses!), all of the other stuff in the forwarded email you received has been left behind. Yeah!

-If you were copying text from an email that had been forwarded many times, you might have copied all of those marks (> > > >) that were in the other email. Let's get rid of those. Put your cursor right before them and click once. Now, hit the Delete key on your keyboard until they are all gone. Keep doing this until you've deleted all of them.

-Now look at your message. You've gotten rid of those funny marks but are there spaces between some of the sentences now? Do they look disjointed? You can clean up empty space by deleting it, just as you deleted the > > > marks. Place your cursor behind the last word of a disjointed sentence and click once. Then, hit the Delete key on your keyboard until the rest of the sentence is joined with the first part. Keep doing this until you've joined all of the disjointed sentences. If you happen to delete something that you didn't want to delete, remember that you can use the shortcut keys, Ctrl + z, to undo your mistake.

-If you want to align the text that you have cleaned up, highlight all of it and then click the align button that you want to use. Maybe you want to change the font, font size, or font color. You can do any of these things and make this new message look any way you want. You now have a fresh, clean, easy to read, and pleasant to look at email message that anyone would be delighted to receive. Would you like to put in a few words to the friends you're sending the message to?

-Move your cursor to right before the first letter of this new text and click once. Hit the Enter key on your keyboard several times.

-Now, click in the white area above the new text and type whatever you want to add.

-Type an appropriate title for your new message in the Subject: box.

-Enter your friends' addresses in the Bcc: box and click Send.

Some people may think that cleaning up emails and hiding addresses is a lot of work and a waste of time. It is, of course, up to you whether or not you want to take the time to do this. I can only go by my own experience. I've gotten so that I simply delete a forwarded email, if it is cluttered, difficult to read, and I have to search for the intended message. My time is valuable, and I'm sure yours is, also. So, do your friends a favor and take the time to clean up those difficult to read emails. They will love you for it!

Reformatting, Saving, and Printing Special Emails

Have you ever received an inspiring or fun email from a friend that you loved so much that you wanted to save it or print it out? You can save emails in different folders in any email program. You can also print them out directly from the message window. Sometimes, though, if the message has been forwarded many times and you want to print it out from the email message window, you will end up printing all of the email clutter, too. Next, you'll learn how to reformat, save, and then print out these favorite emails.

I have a friend, Sandi, whom often emails fun, inspiring, encouraging, and motivational quotes and passages that she loves. I love getting them and I like to reformat them and save them so that I can print them out at different times for other friends who don't have email. I also like to do this so that I can go back and read them whenever I want to. We are going to practice doing this now. If you don't have a special email message that you want to reformat and save, just pick an email that you've received recently and still have in your Inbox to practice with. You can use the steps we are about do with any email program. Remember to Work Offline while we are doing this project.

-First, highlight and Copy (Ctrl + c) the text in the message that you want to reformat. We just learned how to do this with forwarded messages, remember?

-Now, click once on the Start button in the lower left-hand corner of your screen. We are going to open up a new Word document, so move your pointer up to Programs and then across to the next menu. Find and click once on Microsoft Word.

-You'll now be in a new document window. Click once inside the new document area first and then click once on the Paste button on the top middle toolbar to insert your copied text. You should now see the text that you copied from your email message. Think about what font you would like to use for this special message.

-Click once on the Edit button on the top toolbar and then find and click once on Select All. The text will now be highlighted in a dark color.

-Choose and then click on the font, font size, and font color that you have decided on for the text. Would you like the text to be Bold or Italic? How do you want the text to be aligned? When you've made your choices, click in the document area again to remove the highlighting.

-If you need to, you can now clean up the message. Are there those funny marks (> > >)? You can delete them just as you did before. Are the sentences disjointed? Remember that you can clean up the empty spaces, also. When you've finished, let's save this new document that you have just formatted to look beautiful. I have created a special folder, within the My Documents folder, and I save all of my specially formatted fun and inspirational email messages in it. After we save this document, I'll show you how to set up a new folder for your special emails.

-Click File on the top toolbar and then find and click once on Save as.... The Save as window will open up. Look in the Save in: white box at the top of this window. Does it say My Documents? If it doesn't, you can click the yellow folder with the up pointing arrow, tooltip Up One Level, to the right of it to find the folder. When you see the My Documents folder, double click on it or you can save it in another folder if you would like to.

-Decide on a name for your new Word document. In the File name: box delete the phrase that is now in it and type in the new name you've decided on. When you're done, click once on the Save button. Now, close this new Word document by clicking once on the Close button in the top right-hand corner. Then, close your email program.

-Now, you're back at your desktop. Find the My Documents icon shortcut on your desktop. Remember the icons run down the left side of the screen. When you've found the icon, double click on it to open this window. If you don't have the shortcut icon for My Documents on your desktop, double click on the My Computer icon, then double click on (C:), and then double click on My Documents to open up the My Documents window.

-Find and click once on the File button on the top toolbar. Highlight New with your pointer and then slide your pointer over to the new menu and click once on Folder.

-Look in the window file area and you'll see a that a new folder icon titled New Folder, has been added to the list. If the title New Folder is highlighted and in a box, go to the next step. If the title New Folder isn't highlighted, hold your pointer over it and right click your mouse if you are right-handed or left click if you are left-handed. A new menu will pop up. Look towards the bottom of the menu and then find and click once on Rename.

-You'll notice that the New Folder title is now highlighted and in a little box. Hit the Delete key on your keyboard. Now, you'll see a little box with a blinking bar. Let's name this new folder Special Emails or something similar. Type your new folder name and then hit the Enter key on your keyboard once. Great!

-Now we want to put the document that you just saved, with the special and reformatted email message, in this new folder that you've just set up. This next step is one we did before in the Desktop Themes chapter.

-Find the document with the special email on the file list. Hold your pointer over it and then click and hold the mouse button down. Move your pointer, while holding the mouse button down, and position it directly over the new folder you just set up. Now release the mouse button. As you moved the pointer you probably saw, once again, a black circle with a black line through it light up for a moment and what looked like a shadow of the document under the pointer. Your document is now in your new folder.

-To view it, just double click on the new folder. Now, the next time you reformat a special email message, you'll be able to save it in this new folder that you just set up. When you click on Save As...on the File menu, instead of saving it to the My Documents folder double click on your new folder to open it up and then save your new document in it.

-If you have a printer, open this document back up by double clicking on it. We are going to practice printing it out.

-There is a print icon that looks like a little printer on the left side of your middle toolbar that you can use to print. I usually don't use this option, though, because it doesn't give you any control over what is printed or how many copies you may want to print. For instance, if your document is three pages long and you only want to print one of the pages and you want to print multiple copies of this one page, you can't control this if you click on this icon. I'll show you the best way to print out a document.

-First, let's do a print preview. This is a necessity, especially if you have changed the margins in your document. The print preview will show you exactly what will print from your printer. If you've set the margins outside the area that your printer can print, you'll be able to see this in the preview window and change it. Click once on the File button on the top toolbar. Look down the menu and find and click once on Print Preview.

-The Preview window will open up and you'll be able to see your document in a smaller view so that you can check the borders. If you want to see a larger view, just click on the down arrow in the Zoom box and choose 75%. When you're satisfied that the document will print out fine, find and click on the Close button on the middle toolbar. The tooltip for this button is Close Preview.

-Click once on the File button again and this time find and click once on Print to open up the Print window.

-You'll see the titles Printer, Page range, Copies, Print what:, and Print:. Take some time later to check out the Properties button and Options button. Under Page range, click in the white circle next to Current page. Next to Print what:, make sure that it says Document. Under Copies, make sure that the Number of copies is set at 1 if you only want to print one copy. If you want to print more copies, you can use the up/ down arrows to change the number. Next to Print:, make sure it says All pages in range. Now, you're ready to print. Click once on the OK button. If you haven't turned on your printer yet, the computer will probably do it for you or prompt you to turn it on. Great! You've just printed out your special document.

Highlighting Text

Let's take a detour for a minute to find out some other ways to high-light a word, a line of text, a paragraph or the whole body of text, that's a little easier to do than what we did earlier. There are several different ways to do it in your email program or if you are working on a Word document. You can highlight text to change the font, the color of the font, the font size, make it bold, italic, underline it, cut and paste it to move it to another part of your document, delete it, copy it, and center or align it. Whew! There are so many things you can do!

-If you want to change all of the text in an email message or in a Word document, look on the top toolbar, next to File and find the Edit button. Click once on the Edit button and find Select All on the menu. If you click once on Select All, it will highlight the whole body of text.

-Another way to highlight the whole body of text in a Word document only is to move your cursor bar to the far left and very top of the text you want highlighted. Keep moving it left until it turns into an arrow. When you see the arrow, click three times. Your whole body of text should now be highlighted. This also works in some email programs like Hotmail.

-If you want to highlight a word, put your cursor bar right before the word or right on top of the word and click two times. This applies to text in an email message and a Word document.

-If you want to highlight a whole line of text in a Word document, put your cursor bar to the far left of the line you want to change until it changes into an arrow and click one time.

- If you want to highlight a whole line of text in an Outlook email message, move your cursor to the far left of the line you want to highlight, click your mouse button and hold, and then move your mouse over the entire line of text.

-If you want to highlight a paragraph in a Word document, put your cursor bar to the far left of the top line of the paragraph until it changes into an arrow and click two times.

-If you want to highlight a paragraph in an Outlook email message, move your cursor to the far left of the top line of the paragraph and click three times.

Setting Up Other Email Accounts

Setting up other email accounts is an option that I'd like to tell you about and have you consider if you don't already have others set up. At my last job, I had someone help me set up a free email account at Hotmail. My brother and his family had a computer and I wanted to try and learn how to email them. I wasn't able to use the email address at the place that I worked for personal use and I could access the Hotmail account anywhere I could use a computer. So, I had this email account in place when I left my job. If I wanted to email my family, I could go to the local library and use one of their computers. I didn't do this very often, though, because my fear of computers was still pretty big at this point and I hadn't purchased my computer yet.

When I first got my computer, I set up my email account and address with my ISP through the email program that I had installed on my computer, that being Outlook Express. Then, I had two email accounts. Just for practice and when I felt brave enough, I started going on the Internet and searching for general things. When my confidence grew, I began searching for more specific things. Sometimes I would visit a website and want more information, but I really didn't want to give my Outlook Express address. I had decided that it would be my private address and I only gave it out to my friends and family. I had also heard, that if a site wasn't secure, your information and email address could be put on a mailing list and then you would probably start getting lots of junk email. So, I decided that my Hotmail account would be my email information address. Now, whenever I visit a site and they ask for an email address, I give them my Hotmail address. I do get junk mail, but at least it isn't showing up at my private email address. And...if there is ever a serious problem with email that I am receiving at this account, I can close it very easily and open up a new account.

When I decided to do a fun website about Sherwood, I wanted people to be able to email me about Sherwood. I didn't want to put my private email address on the website. Also, I really wanted to keep emails
that I got about the website separate from my email information
address. So, I set up a third email address at Yahoo since that's where I
had my free website space. This email address is just for Sherwood and
it's free, also. Then, I put the addresses for my Hotmail and Yahoo mail
accounts in my Internet Explorer Favorites file so that I could easily
access them everyday without having to type in the address.

If you have just one email address at this point, and have been having
a problem with using your email address at websites, you might consider setting up a free email account in addition to the one you already
have. There are many places on the Internet now where you can do this.
Two of the most popular are Yahoo Mail at yahoo.com and Hotmail at
msn.com. They provide instructions at their websites on how to set up
free accounts. Another nice thing about having another email account
set up, that isn't through your ISP, is that if you are traveling and can get
to a computer, you can keep in contact with friends and family by having them email you at your free account address. So take some time and
think about this option.

Finding Outlook Express Stationery

You can search for new Outlook Express Stationery just as you would
anything else. Whenever you are searching, just type Outlook Express
Stationery in the search box and click the search button. Check out
yahoo.com, msn.com, snap.com, or any other search site that you know
of. Be sure to visit ringsurf.com to surf some stationery webrings. Also,
Microsoft, at microsoft.com, frequently has free updates on the programs that are installed with Windows. You can search at their website
for stationery and many other things as well.

Sending Free Egreeting Cards

Here are some website addresses for free ecards that you can pick out and have emailed to your friends. All Yours at all-yours.net, Oh Angel at ohangel.com, House Mouse Designs at house-mouse.com, Castle Mountains Cards at castlemountains.com, Blue Mountain Cards at bluemountain.com, Zing Cards at zing.com, Send 4 Fun at send4fun.com, and American Greetings at americangreetings.com. These are just of few of the many egreeting websites on the Internet. You can go to these websites and select a card from a wide selection and then type in whatever you want to say to your friends. Some of these websites also allow you to play music with the card. You can also search for more egreetings sites at search sites and webrings.

                    *   *   *   *   *   *

We've covered a lot in this chapter. Do you feel more accomplished? You should, you've worked hard! The neat thing is that it probably didn't feel like work did it? I love to learn by playing, experimenting, and being creative. We're going to do some more fun projects in the next chapter, so let your imagination run wild while you consider all the different ways you can use the skills that you will be learning.

6

Lets Play Some More

Are you ready to play some more? Have you been having fun? Do you feel as though you now have some very important computer skills? I hope so, because you do. We're now going to learn some more skills by experimenting and being creative. This chapter will consist of fun projects that you can do in your Microsoft Word program. As you do each one, remember to consider the possibilities.

I like to use Microsoft Word for all of my projects because I feel that I have more creative freedom. If you would like something more structured, Microsoft Works is a good program to check out. It has templates installed for everything from stationery to gift tags that you can use.

Do you have a color printer? I want to take a moment and cover the topic of printers. When I was thinking about buying my computer, the thought of getting a printer didn't even occur to me. When I was talking with the sales rep from Gateway about the Astro model I ended up buying and how little space it took, he mentioned that I might want to consider getting a color printer, also. At that time, I didn't realize all of the creative things that I could do on my computer. At first, I really resisted the idea of getting a printer. I thought that printers were very expensive and I really couldn't see the advantages of having one. We talked some more and what finally sold me on the idea of a printer was the price. It was much less expensive than I thought it would be. Granted, I wasn't ordering a really fancy model. The one I decided on was a small inexpensive color deskjet model from Hewlett Packard. It was one of the wisest choices I could have made. I use my little color printer So Much! Now, I can't imagine being without it. Most of what I print out are the colorful creative projects that I love to do. But it's also great for printing out all of the text documents that I make. So, if you don't have a printer and you love being creative, you might want to consider getting one. I imagine that if you do purchase one, you'll be glad you did.

We've gone over how to use clip art files that you have on your computer, clip art files on the Greetings CD, and how to find clip art on the Internet. What if you have pictures or artwork, that isn't on your computer, that you'd like to use in the creative projects that you make on your computer? You can scan them! I don't have a scanner, because I definitely don't have the room for it right now. And, because, I have a lot of clip art close at hand to use. But sometimes I do want to scan a photo or piece of artwork. If this is the case, I take the picture or artwork to a local copying store that has graphic design services. They will scan pictures for me for a very nominal fee. So, if you don't have a scanner and would like to have something scanned, check with your local copier stores to see if they provide this service or find a friend who has a scanner. You'll need to take floppy discs with you for them to copy the scanned image onto. If it is a large graphics file, they may have to scan it on to a zip disc. Another possibility is to have them copy the graphics on a CD for you, if you don't have a zip drive. When you have the image on your floppy, zip, or CD disc, just pop it into the disc drive on your computer and copy it into one of your folders. Then you can create your project with the image that you've had scanned.

Fun and Simple Business Cards

Are you starting a new business and don't really have any money in your budget to do a large run of business cards? Maybe you'd like to let people know about an upcoming event and you don't want to make up large flyers. Maybe you just want to make small cards for whatever reason. When I finished my Sherwood website, I wanted to be able to give people something small, like a business card, that let them know about the website and also had the website address on it. I didn't want to have them done at a copy store because I didn't need very many done up. So, I decided I would make my own! I went to a local specialty stationery store and bought 5 sheets of 8 ½ x 11 lightweight card stock paper. After I designed my cards, I printed them out on the special paper and then cut them out. Then, I gave them out to people so they could go and see Sherwood.

Next, we're going to do a card project for simple business cards in Microsoft Word so that you can practice. We're going to be making business cards for a fictional restaurant called Blue Sky Cafe. Remember that if you don't have a printer you can still print the cards we are about to design. If you have a friend who has a printer, you can email the document as an attachment to him/ her to print out. If you don't remember how to do this, just refer to the chapter, Email Magic.

-Open up a new document in Word by clicking on Start, moving your pointer up to Programs, moving over to the next menu and then clicking once on Microsoft Word.

-We need to adjust the margins, so find and click once on the File button on the top toolbar. Move your pointer down to and click once on Page Setup…to open up the Page Setup window.

-You'll see the tabs Margins, Paper Size, Paper Source, and Layout. Make sure you are in the Margins tab window. Set the Top:, Bottom:, Left:, and Right: margins to 0.5 by clicking on the little down arrows.

-Next, find and click once on the Paper Size tab. Then, find and click in the white circle next to Landscape under Orientation. Make sure that the white box next to Apply to: says Whole document. Click once on the OK button to return to your document. Your document page will now be in the Landscape position.

-We're going to be working in a smaller view for a few moments. Find the Zoom menu on the toolbar above your document. Click on the down arrow and then find and click once on 50%.

-Next, we are going to insert a 3 x 3 table. We'll be using the table in the background so that we have some guidelines to follow when we are sizing the cards. So, look up to the toolbar that is above the alignment buttons on the font toolbar. You'll see a little icon that looks kind of like a calendar. Hold your pointer over it to see the tooltip. It should say Insert Table. Click once on this button.

-The menu with white boxes you now see will allow you to choose how many rows and columns you want in your table. We want 3 columns across and 3 rows down. Move your pointer over the boxes to highlight them. When you've highlighted the boxes and it says 3 x 3 Table at the bottom, click your mouse button once to insert the 3 x 3 table into your document.

-Place your cursor over the bottom line of the table. Do you see that it has now changed into an up/ down arrow ↕ with a double line = in between the arrows? When you see this up/ down arrow, click your mouse button and hold it. You'll now see a dotted line that extends all of the way across your window. This feature allows you to move the line up or down. We want to move the bottom line all the way down to just before the bottom margin.

-Look at the ruler on the left-hand side of your document. The white area is the area within the margin. The dark area is where the margin stops. The bottom margin for your document area should end at approximately 7 ½ if you set all of your margins at 0.5. Take a moment to check your bottom margin. We are going to move the bottom line of the table to just before 7 ½ on the ruler.

-Click and hold your mouse button on the bottom line when you see the up/ down arrow. This next part is a little tricky. Move your mouse down slowly until you see that the dotted line is right before 7 ½ on the left ruler. Release your mouse button. You'll now see a row of big table cells and two rows of small cells. Next, we need to distribute the rows evenly.

-Position your cursor above the far left column of the table and then move your cursor slowly down over the top line of the table until you see this down arrow ⬇. When you see the arrow, click and hold your mouse button and slide your mouse down and across the table until you see that all three columns are highlighted black. It won't completely highlight the bottom row. Release your mouse button.

-Now, find and click once on the Table button on the top toolbar. Move your pointer down and click once on Distribute Rows Evenly. Your table should now have evenly spaced rows and columns. Leave the table highlighted for a moment. We are going to fade out the border lines for the table.

-On the font toolbar, right above the document, you'll see a square divided into four smaller squares to the left of, A, the button for font color. The tooltip for this icon is All Borders. Click the down arrow to the right of it to view the border menu. In the lower right-hand corner, you'll see a square with all dotted gray lines. Hold your pointer over it to view the tooltip No Border. Click once on this button to fade out the border lines on your table. Click back in the document area once to remove the highlight. Your table should now have light gray lines.

-Let's stop here for a moment and Save this document. Click once on the File button on your top toolbar and then find and click on Save As…to open up your Save As window. Find the folder that you want to save this file in. My Documents is a good one. Delete the highlighted word in the File name: box and type in Fun business cards. Now, click once on the Save button. Remember that you should always save the changes that you have made to your work periodically.

-Now, change the Zoom level of your document to 75%. We're going to design the business card for Blue Sky Cafe!

-Look on your bottom toolbar and find the icon to the left of WordArt. The tooltip will be Text Box. Click the button once.

-Move your pointer up to the top left square of your table, it will change into a different cursor that looks like this +. Click inside the top left square to insert your Text box.

-Position your cursor over each of the up/ down/ right/ left white boxes and then click, hold and move your mouse to size the text box. Use the gray lines of this first square as your guide. You want to size the text box so that each side is right before the gray line.

-Click inside the text box. You should now see a small blinking bar. Check your font. Does it say Times New Roman size 10? If it doesn't, change it to this font setting for a moment. This font size will allow you to space down, without enlarging the text box, to the middle of the card so we can type in the information.

-Find and click once on the Center alignment button to center the blinking bar.

-Hit the Enter key on your keyboard five times to move the blinking bar to the center of the text box.

-Now, change your font to Cooper Black, font size 14, and font color light blue.

-Type Great Food! Hit the Enter key once. Type Great Atmosphere! Hit the Enter key once. Type Great Waitpeople! Stop. Don't hit the Enter key yet.

-Now, change the font to Comic Sans, font size 12, font color red. Hit the Enter key once.

-Now, type 1111 Gateway Lane. Hit the Enter key once. Next, type Anytown, USA. Hit the Enter key once. Finally, type 222-234-5678. Now, let's put a border around your card.

-Look on the bottom toolbar and find the paint brush tip icon. Click the down arrow to view the color menu. Find and click on the light blue color box that we used for the font color.

-Next, click once on the lines with the tooltip Line Style to the right of the A on the bottom toolbar. Look for the two thin lines with 3 pt to the left of them. Click once on the two thin lines. Your card should now have a light blue, double lined border. Great!

-Let's do a colorful WordArt title for our card. Find and click once on the floating A WordArt icon on the bottom toolbar to open up the WordArt Gallery window.

-Click once on the top left-hand corner Style box and then click the OK button. This will open up the Edit Word Text window.

-Hit the Delete key on your keyboard to remove Your Text Here from the Text: area.

-Choose the font Cooper Black and the font size 20. Click inside the Text: area and type Blue Sky Cafe. Click once on the OK button to insert the WordArt into your document area.

-Place your cursor over Blue Sky Cafe until you see the four-sided arrow. When you do, click and hold your mouse button and then move your mouse and position your WordArt in the blank space above Great Food! on your card. Size the WordArt phrase to fill the blank space.

-Now, let's fill the WordArt and give it a new shape. Click once on the paint can button in the small WordArt window with the tooltip, Format WordArt, to open up that window. Click on the down arrow next to the Color: box and then click on Fill Effects…to open that window.

-Click in the white circle next to Preset. Choose Daybreak from the drop down Preset colors: menu. Under Shading Styles, click in the white circle next to Horizontal. Under Variants, find and click on the lower left-hand box that has the white color running through the center. Now, click the OK button to return to the Format WordArt window.

-Under Line: you'll see Color:. From the drop down color menu to the right of it, click on the light blue color that we used for the border of our card. Next to Dashed:, choose the solid line from the drop down menu. From the Weight: menu choose 0.75 by clicking the up/ down arrows. Next, click once on the OK button.

-Now, lets change the shape of the WordArt phrase. Click once on the Abc button with the tooltip, WordArt shape, next to the paint can icon in the small WordArt window. We are going to use the Inflate Top shape. It's in the fourth row down and the fifth shape over from the left. Hold your pointer over the shape to see the tooltip. Click once on the Inflate Top button to shape your WordArt.

Hey, you've just designed a business card! This is a very simple one. Later, if you want to, you can get more elaborate by inserting Autoshapes, symbols, or clip art. Now, we need to fill the document page with more cards. With this size of card we will be able to get nine cards to a page, since we set up the table to have nine cells. If you want to make smaller or larger cards, just adjust the number of cells in the table that you insert. The size that we are using now is approximately the same size as a regular business card.

-Click once on the card we just made. You should see the white boxes on the outside border. Move your pointer up to top middle toolbar and find and click once on the Copy button. It's in between the Cut and Paste buttons. Your card has now been copied onto your computer's Clipboard until you paste it somewhere. You can't see it, but it's there.

-Place your cursor in the empty cell next to the card and click once. Now, go back up to the top middle toolbar and find and click once on the Paste button. You'll now see a second card, minus the WordArt, on top of the first card.

-Place your cursor over the second card until you see the four-sided arrow. When you do, click and hold your mouse button. Now, move your mouse to position the second card in the empty cell next to the first card.

-Click in the empty cell next to the second card. Go back to the Paste button and click once. Your third card will now be on top of the first

card again. Move and position it in the third empty cell. Repeat these
steps until you have nine cards filling the nine empty cells.

-Now we need to copy the WordArt phrase Blue Sky Cafe. We're
going to do this copy job a little differently. Click once on the phrase
in the first card. You should now see the white boxes on the outside of
the title Blue Sky Cafe. Move your pointer up and click on the Copy
button once.

-Let's finish the top row first. We need two more titles to finish the
top row. So, move your pointer up to Paste and click on it twice, slowly.
You now have two more WordArt titles. Move each of them into position on the two top cards.

-Click once on one of the titles so that you see the white boxes. We
need three more titles for the second row. Go back to the Paste button
and click it slowly three times. Position these three titles. Finish your
project by copying and positioning the last three titles into place.

-Now, look at your cards. Do you see a squiggly line underneath the
words Waitpeople and Anytown? If your options are set up to check
your spelling and grammar as you are typing, your computer will put
these squiggly lines under words it is not sure about. If you see these
lines, let's do the spell and grammar check before we save the changes
that we've made.

-Click once on the Tools button on the top toolbar. Move your
pointer down to and click once on Spelling and Grammar...to open up
this window. You'll see Waitpeople first in the white box. Click once on
the button titled Ignore All. If you click on Ignore, it will check all nine
cards for the word Waitpeople. Do the same for Anytown.

-Whenever you do the spell and grammar check, you can change
mistakes that you've made by finding and clicking once on the correct
option in the lower white box under Suggestions:. Then click once on
the Change button. If the option isn't in the lower white box, you can
click inside the top white box and delete your mistake and retype it.
Then, click once on the Change button.

-Click once on Save on the File menu to save the changes that you have made to your Business Card document. I would suggest keeping this file as a template. Meaning, anytime that you want to do a card project with cards this size, you can open this document, delete eight of the cards, redesign the first card and then recopy and position them into place. This way, you won't have to start from scratch with the table, etc.

-Now you're ready to print your great new cards! Click once on the File button, and then once again on Print Preview to make sure that all of your borders are within the printing area. Click the Close button to return to your document. If you see that one of the borders is not showing in the Print Preview, you can adjust that card now.

-Anytime you do a special project like this, you should print one practice page. You can do that now on regular printing paper. Find and click once on Print...on the File menu. Choose Current page, Document, 1 copy, and All pages in range. Then click once on the OK button to print out your practice sheet of cards.

-If you're satisfied with the printing of your cards, put your special card stock paper in the printer and print away!

You can make any size cards using these steps. Just set up the table on your document page and choose the number of cells you want shown on the page to use as guidelines. You could even make small folded cards, like place card name tents. Or, you could make a large folded card to set on a table with an announcement attractively printed on it. If your printer is set up to print on both sides of a page, greeting cards can also me made this way by setting up the table with two large cells to use as guidelines.

Simple and Fun Stickers

I'm sure you've seen the Avery labels that you can buy to make address labels and name tags. You can also buy sheets of Avery paper that have no cut outs on them at your local copy store. These are great for designing your own stickers. Once the stickers have been printed on the Avery paper you'll need to cut them out yourself, though. To find out how to print on Avery paper with your printer, find your printer manual and look for information on printing labels onto Avery paper. The process for printing your own stickers will be basically the same as printing labels with this special kind of paper. You'll just need to know which side of the paper goes up on your printer.

What would you use these for? Maybe you're a teacher and would like to find inventive ways to praise your students that would reflect your creativity. Maybe you're having an important meeting next week and you want to design really interesting name tags for all of the people who will be attending. Perhaps everyone in your office has been really stressed lately and you would like to make some fun stickers for everyone to wear tomorrow to help lighten the mood. I've got heart stickers that I keep in my wallet. For many years I waitressed, so I know how difficult this job can be when you're very busy. Now, if I see that a waitperson is not having a good day, I'll leave a heart sticker for them with the tip to try and brighten their day. You can use stickers for anything and for everyone. Let's practice making some now.

-First you need to open up a new document in Microsoft Word. Click on Start, move your pointer up to Programs, and then find and click once on Microsoft Word.

-Click on File on the top toolbar and then find and click on Page Setup…. In the Page Setup window under the Margins tab, set your Top:, Bottom:, Left:, and Right: margins to 0.5. Under the Paper Size tab, click in the white circle next to Portrait under Orientation. Click once on the OK button to return to your document.

-Click on the File button again and then find and click once on Save As…. Save this new document in the folder of your choice by double clicking on the folder and then typing in the new name, Fun stickers, next to File name:. Click once on the Save button to save your new file and to return to your new document.

-Find and click once on 75% in the Zoom drop down menu. With the document set at this size you will be able to get an accurate idea of the size of each sticker that you will be making. This window will show the page at approximately the same size as an 8 ½ x 11 piece of paper. As you are making the stickers, watch the top and left ruler to make sure that you are keeping the sticker in the margin area of your document so that all of it will print. If you are unsure about whether or not a sticker is within the print margin, check your Print Preview to see for sure.

-Let's make a heart sticker first. Find and click once on the AutoShapes button on your bottom toolbar. Move your pointer up to Basic Shapes and then across to the shape menu. Find and click once on the heart button. Move your cursor, which will now look like this +, up to the top left of your document and click it once.

-Now, size the heart. Place your cursor over one of the white boxes until you see the two-sided arrow. Click, hold, and then move your mouse to size the heart. Note: Here's a neat feature that you can apply to all of the AutoShapes. Let's say that you decided at the end of this project to make a whole page of heart stickers. To make the most of the space on the page, you can rotate the hearts, as well as any AutoShape, to make more room. Click once on the heart. Now, find and click once on the circling arrow, tooltip Free Rotate, on the far left of the bottom toolbar. You'll notice that the white boxes around the heart have now turned into green circles. You can click and hold your pointer on any of the green circles and move your mouse to rotate the heart. To remove the free rotate option, click on the Free Rotate button again on the bottom toolbar.

-Click on the down arrow next to the paint can on the bottom tool-bar to view the color menu. Find and click on Fill Effects. In the Fill Effects window, under the Gradient tab, find Colors and then click in the white circle next to One color.

-Under Color 1: click the down arrow, find and click on More colors at the bottom of this menu. What color would you like for the heart to be? I chose a pinkish red color. Click once on the OK button, after you've chosen your color, to return to the Fill Effects window.

-Under Shading Styles, find and click in the white circle next to From center.

-Under the Color 1: box, you'll see the titles Dark and Light. Click the right and left pointing arrows to view how the color that you chose changes. How do you want your heart to look? When you have decided on your dark/ light color preference, click on the color box that you like the best under Variants and then click once on the OK button to return to your document.

-Find and click on the down arrow next to the paintbrush tip on the bottom toolbar. Choose a color for the border around the heart that compliments and is darker than the color you chose for the heart. Click once on the OK button to return to the document.

-Now, click once on the lines, tooltip Line Style, that are to the right of the A on the bottom toolbar. Click once on the 3 pt solid line.

-Next, let's do a WordArt phrase for the center of the heart. Click on the WordArt icon on the bottom toolbar. Look for the box with the wavy WordArt phrase that is four boxes down from the top left and four boxes across. When you find it, click once on it to open up the Edit WordArt text window.

-Hit your Delete key to remove Your Text Here. Choose the font Snap ITC, the font size 16, click in the Text: area and type I'm Special! Click once on the OK button to return to your document. Now, move the WordArt to the center of the heart.

-The WordArt that we chose has a shadow. You can adjust this feature in a moment if you want to, but first choose a color for your font by clicking once on the paint can in the small WordArt window. Under Fill, click the down arrow next to the Color: box and click once on a color. Under line, click the down arrow next to the Color: box and click once on a color. You can set the line and weight to your preference. Click once on the OK button to return to the document.

-Take a few moments and size your WordArt. Do you see the two little yellow diamonds near the white boxes around the WordArt? Play with these for a few minutes. Your cursor will change to a small white arrow when you place it over one of these diamonds. Click and hold your mouse button and move it slightly and then release it. The phrase has now changed in appearance. Find a shape that you like or leave it as is.

-Now, do you want to keep the shadow behind the phrase I Am Special!? If you would like to remove it, click on the shadow box icon, tooltip Shadow, on the bottom toolbar. Find and click on the No Shadow button at the top of the shadow menu to remove the shadow.

-If you would like to keep the shadow, you can change the way it is placed and the color of it. Click on the shadow box icon on the bottom toolbar and experiment with the different shadow styles that are listed on the menu by clicking once on them.

-If you would like to change the color of the shadow, find and click on Shadow Settings…on the Shadow menu. Click the down arrow on the right side of the Shadow Settings window to choose a color from the color menu. You can make the shadow semitransparent if you would like.

-You can also tweak and adjust the shadow more if you want to in the Shadow Settings window, by clicking on one of the four shadow boxes with arrows. Hold your pointer over each one to see the tooltips Nudge Shadow Up, Down, Right and Left. Click once on the Close button in the Shadow Settings window to close it, when you have made your shadow choices.

Your heart sticker is done. What do you think? Children love these heart stickers. I bet if you gave one to an adult to wear, it would make them smile, too. Maybe you need a heart sticker to wear right now. Or you could put it on your computer, next to your screen, where you can see it everyday!

-Next, let's try an interesting looking name tag. Click once on the AutoShapes button on the bottom toolbar, move your pointer up to Basic Shapes and across to the next menu. Find and click on the shape with the tooltip Octagon. Move your cursor up next to the heart and click once to insert the octagon. Size the octagon to your preference.

-We're going to fill the octagon with a texture, so click on the down arrow next to the paint can to open up the color menu and then find and click on Fill Effects…. Click once on the Texture tab and then scroll down the menu to find the box that looks like water droplets. Click once on this box and then click the OK button to close the window. Wow, a water droplet name tag!

-Now, click on the down arrow next to the paintbrush tip to find a line border color that will go with this texture.

-Next, click on the lines with the tooltip Line Style and then click on the 4 ½ pt solid line.

-Do you want to add a line in the middle of the name tag or leave it blank? If you want to add a line, click once on the diagonal line with the tooltip Line next to AutoShapes on the bottom toolbar.

-Now, move your cursor up to the name tag. Click your mouse button, hold it, and then move your mouse to draw the line. Release the mouse button.

-To make it longer, click and hold your cursor, when it turns into a two-sided arrow, on one of the white boxes at the end of the line. Move your mouse to make the line longer. If you want to move the line, click and hold your mouse button when you see the four-sided arrow and then move your mouse to move the line.

-When you have sized and positioned the line, click on the down arrow next to the paint brush tip to choose a line color. Then, click on the Line button to choose a Line Style. People will be impressed when they see your custom made name tags!

-For our next practice sticker, let's make a really fun one. Click once on AutoShapes on the bottom menu. Move your pointer up to Basic Shapes and then find and click once on the Lightening Bolt button. Move your cursor next to the octagon or below it, in the document area, and click once to insert the lightening bolt.

-Now, rotate the lightening bolt by clicking on the Free Rotate button on the bottom toolbar. Click and hold your mouse button over one of the green circles and then move your mouse to rotate the lightening bolt. Move the bolt so that the end point of it is angled to the left. Click once again on the Free Rotate button to remove this feature.

-Next, size the bolt. You'll need to make this sticker a little larger than the others, so that when we put a WordArt phrase on it there will be room for the words. I made mine about 4 inches long by 1 ½ inches wide.

-Now, let's fill it with a wild pattern. Click on the down arrow next to the paint can and then click on Fill Effects…. Click once on the Pattern tab. Under Patterns: find and click on the box in the top row, sixth from the left that has zig zag lines.

-Under Foreground:, click the down arrow and then click on the white color box. Under Background:, click the down arrow and then click on the gold color box. Click once on the OK button to apply the pattern.

-Next, click on the down arrow next to the paintbrush tip and click on a bright red color box. Then click on the Line Style lines and click on the 2 ¼ pt solid line. Snazzy!

-It's time for WordArt! Click on the WordArt button to open the WordArt Gallery window. Click on the box in the top left-hand corner and then click once on the OK button. Hit the Delete key on your keyboard to remove Your Text Here. Choose the font Bradley Hand ITC, the font size 20, and then click the B button to make the font bold. Click inside the Text: area and type I'm Dazzling! Click once on the OK button to close this window.

-Now, find and click once on the Free Rotate button in the small WordArt window. Click on one of the green circles, hold the mouse button down, and rotate the WordArt phrase so that it is at a diagonal slant and aligned with the lightening bolt. Click on the Free Rotate button again to remove this option. Size the phrase to fit and then move it to the top part of the lightening bolt.

-Click once on the paint can in the small WordArt window and choose the red color you used for the border of the lightening bolt as the Fill color and the Line color. Choose the solid line next to Dashed and for the Weight, choose 3 pt. What do you think? Is the lightening bolt sticker wild enough for you?

For our final sticker, I'm going to give you some initial instructions and then you get to play with it to make it look just the way you want it to.

-Okay! Open the AutoShapes menu and find the 5-Point Star in the Stars and Banners menu. Click once on it and then click in the document below your heart sticker to insert the shape. Size and position the star.

-Pick a fill color or fill effects, line color, and line style for your star.

-What would you like your star sticker to say? Design a WordArt phrase to go inside the star.

-Now, find the three-dimensional box on the bottom toolbar next to the shadow box. The tooltip for it is 3-D. Click once on the 3-D box to see the menu. Choose a 3-D shape for your star sticker and click once on it.

-Click on the 3-D button again and then click on 3-D Settings…at the bottom of the menu. A small 3-D Settings window will open up. If you hold your pointer over each of the buttons you'll see the tooltips, 3-D On/ Off, Tilt Down, Tilt Up, Tilt Left, Tilt Right, Depth, Direction, Lighting, Surface, 3-D Color (Custom).

-Now…Play! Take some time and try out all of the options available to you with 3-D Settings. When you're done playing and you've made your 3-D choices, you can close the 3-D Settings window. I bet your star sticker looks fantastic!

With any of these AutoShapes, you can also add text to the shape by right clicking and choosing Add text on the small menu that pops up. Using WordArt phrases gives you more dimension and choice, though. The great thing about making your own stickers this way is that they will be one of a kind and people will love them. Do you remember how to print out your page? If you don't, you can refer back to the directions at the end of the fun business card section. Always print a practice page before printing your stickers onto the Avery paper. What kind of fun stickers can you come up with?

Word Banners

We're going to make interesting word banners next. They're great to use for posters, bulletin boards, or anything that you need a sign for. I recently made a dream poster to hang on the wall above my computer where I can see it everyday. I found clip art pictures that represented the different aspects of my dream home, garden, etc., on the Internet. Then I saved them in my picture file, inserted them into a new document, sized them, and printed them out. Then I went wild and made lots of colorful and inspiring word banners to put on my poster. When I was finished, I glued the pictures and word banners on a piece of poster board that was printed with dreamy clouds. Now, when I stretch and flex after working at my computer for a long time, I can look up and see my poster and remember my dreams and smile.

-Okay! Let's open up a new document in Microsoft Word. Find and click once on Page Setup on the File menu, and set the margins for this new document at .5. Then, choose the Landscape orientation under the Paper Size tab. Next, save this new document in your Document folder with the name Word banners. Do you remember how to do these things? If you don't, read through the beginning directions for cards or stickers.

-We are going to make a Text Box word banner first. You'll need to set your Zoom to 50% so that you can see the whole page. After you've done this, take a moment and notice where your margins are so that when you size your text box, you'll be sure to keep it in the margins.

-Find the Text Box button on the bottom toolbar to the left of the floating WordArt A. Click on the button once and then move your cursor up the top left corner of the document page. Your cursor will now look like this +. Click and hold your mouse button and then slowly slide it down and across the page. Release the mouse button and check your margins. You want the word banner to extend all the way across the page and still be within the margins. So, make it approximately 10 inches across and then approximately 2 ½ inches down. Resize now, if you need to.

-Let's fill the banner with a Preset selection. Click once on the down arrow next to the paint can on the bottom toolbar and then once again on Fill Effects…to open up that window. Under the Gradient tab, click once in the circle next to Preset to choose this option and then find and click once on Sapphire from the drop down menu.

-Click in the white circle next to Vertical under Shading styles. Choose and click on one of the bottom boxes under Variants. Click once on the OK button to close this window. What do you think? Doesn't it look majestic?

-Now, click on the down arrow next to the paintbrush tip and click on the gold color box. Click on the Line Style button and then find and click once on the 3 pt solid line from the menu.

-You'll notice that there is a tiny blinking bar in the upper left-hand corner of your text box. Make sure that your font, for the moment, is set at Times New Roman, font size 10. Click on the Center alignment button to center the blinking bar. Hit the Enter key on your keyboard 3 times.

-Now, change your font to Harrington, font size 72. Find and click once on the B button for bold, and the U button for underline. Move your pointer across this toolbar and click on the down arrow next to the A for font color and choose the color white. Now type, I Believe in Miracles!.

Isn't it maaahvelous? (To quote Billy Crystal.) The only drawback with using the text box is that you can't do a whole lot with the text font and font color. But using the text box is great if you want to emphasize a section in a document or on a flyer. You can insert the box between other sections of text and then use different colors to enhance the background so that it will stand out from the body of text. You could also do this same project by using a rectangle AutoShape for the background and then creating the phrase with the WordArt option.

-Okay, let's try another word banner. Find and click on the down arrow next to Autoshapes on the bottom toolbar. Move your pointer up to Stars and Banners and then across to the new menu. In the third row down, second object over you'll see a small ribbon. Hold your pointer over this button to see the tooltip Down Ribbon. Click once on this button.

-Move your pointer up to the left margin and in the area below your first word banner. Click and hold the mouse button and slide your cursor down and across the page. Release the mouse button. Do you see a white banner? We're going to fill it with color in a moment, but first notice the two yellow diamonds. Do you remember using these before with the WordArt phrase, I'm Special!? If you move the yellow diamonds it will alter the shape of the ribbon. Leave the top diamond set. We want more room for the WordArt we are going to put on the ribbon, though, so move the bottom diamond to the left as far as it will go. Now, resize this new banner so that it extends across the page and stays within the margins. You can make it taller, also, if you want to.

-Click the down button next to the paint can on the bottom toolbar and then click once on Fill Effects…to open up that window. Under the Gradient tab, choose Preset and then find and click once on Gold from the drop down menu. Choose the Horizontal shading style. Under

Variants click on the box in the bottom left-hand corner. Click once on the OK button to close this window. Isn't the gold color elegant?

-Let's make the border a dark purple. Click the down arrow next to the paintbrush tip on the bottom toolbar and find this color. Then, click once on the Line Style button and choose the 3 pt solid line.

-Now we're ready for some WordArt. Click the WordArt button on the bottom toolbar to open up that window. Choose the top left-hand box and then click once on the OK button. Hit the Delete key to delete Your Text Here. Choose the font Impact and the font size 24. Click in the Text: area and type the phrase All my hard work. Hit the Enter key once. Then type, will soon pay off!. Click once on the OK button to close that window.

-Now, move the WordArt phrase to the center of the banner. Take a moment to resize it and make it larger. Next, click on the paint can in the small WordArt window to open the Format WordArt window. Click the down arrow under Fill Color: and then click once on Fill Effects....

-Under the Gradient tab click in the white circle before One Color to choose it. Then find and click on the same dark purple that you used for the border in the drop down color menu. Make sure that the small circle next to Horizontal is selected under Shading styles.

-Now, slide the cursor bar towards Light until you see a dark purple and a very light purple in the boxes below. Click on the bottom left-hand corner box that has the light purple color running through the middle. Click once on the OK button to close this window.

-Under Line, click on the dark purple color box again and then choose 1 pt and a solid line. Click once on the OK button to close this window. You're done! And…all of your hard work is paying off already if you've gotten this far in the book.

-To print these banners, check your Print Preview first and then follow the directions given for printing in the fun business card section or near the end of the Email Magic chapter.

There are so many things that you can do with word banners. You can make them really small or really large if you use legal size paper. Or, you can print them on the lightweight card stock paper that we used earlier. You can insert other AutoShapes or clip art to enhance your word banners, also. Experiment on your own and have fun.

This next section is for future reference. What if you've created a document that has pictures or graphics and you also want to type in text? An example of this would be if you were making a flyer that had a picture or graphic at the top and then text below it. If you are working on a project like this, you will need to format the picture or graphic so that you can place the typed text where you want it on the document page. To do this…

-Click once on the picture or graphic (i.e.,WordArt, Autoshape, etc.)

-Then, click once on the Format button on the top toolbar. Look towards the bottom of the small menu that pops down. If you are formatting a picture, it will say Picture. If you are formatting a graphic, it will say Object. Click once on either Picture or Object.

-The Format Picture or Format Object window will open up. Find the Position tab and click once on it. To keep the picture/ object in place and so that it won't move with the text that you type in on the document page, make sure that the white box next to Move object with text doesn't have a check in it. If it does, click once inside the box to remove the check.

-Make sure that the box next to Float over text does have a check in it. This will make it easier to position your picture/ object on the document page.

-Next, click once on the Wrapping tab. The choices you make here will allow you to place text around, above or below, or to the sides of your picture.

-Under Wrapping style, choose the wrapping style that you want for your text and click once on it. For instance, if you choose Tight, then under Wrap to you can choose were you want the text to be in relation to your picture/object.

-Under Distance from text, you can choose the distance you want between your picture/ object and your text. When you've made your choices, you can click once on the OK button to close this window.

Saving Important Information On Floppy Discs

Do you have important documents/files/folders that you haven't backed up? A very important thing to do once you start compiling and saving information and graphics on your computer is to copy and save important files to a floppy disc or zip disc. If your computer breaks down for whatever reason and your files are wiped out, you will have all your information saved on the floppy disc and you will be able to restore it easily to your computer once it is working again. I don't have a zip drive, so that is an option that I can't use at this time. I am checking into getting one sometime in the future. The reason that I will eventually get a zip drive is because you can save a lot more data on a zip disc than you can on a floppy disc. Another option to consider is a CD burner. With a CD burner you can copy an enormous amount of information onto a CD.

-To copy and save important information onto a floppy disc, put a floppy disc in your disc drive (make sure that the small round metal disc on the floppy is facing down when you insert the floppy) and then double click on the My Computer icon on your Desktop. Now, double click on (C:) to open up that window.

-Find the folder that has the information or graphics that you want to save to the floppy and double click on it to open it (remember that graphics files are large and may not all fit onto a floppy disc.) Now, click once on the document/ file that you want to copy. If you want to save several documents/ files at the same time you can hold down the Ctrl key on your keyboard and then click on the documents/ files that you want to copy. This will highlight all of them.

-Be sure to watch the file size if you are copying several files at once, so that you can be sure that they will all fit onto the floppy. A floppy disc usually has approximately 1.38 to 1.44 MB of space on it. To find out the file size, click once on the file and then look over to the left of the window. You'll see a description of the file and the size listed. If the file is an image file, you will also be able to see a small thumbnail image below this information by moving the scroll bar down. If you're not sure, just copy one document/ file at a time. If your floppy is full, your computer will tell you.

-Find and click once on the Edit button on the top toolbar. Move your pointer down and click once on Copy.

-Now, click on the Back arrow or the folder with the up arrow until you return to the Computer window. You'll see the list of drives, i.e., (A:), (C:), and (D:), as well as a few other folders.

-Double click on 3 ½ Floppy (A:) to open it up. Find and click once on the Edit button on the top toolbar. Move your pointer down and click once on Paste. The documents/ files that you copied will now be pasted and saved onto your floppy disc.

-Anytime you revise or change a file, you will need to recopy it onto this floppy disc. Follow the above directions to copy the revised document/ file and then to paste it onto the floppy disc. If the file you are updating on your floppy disc is in a specific folder, double click on the folder that has the file that you are going to update with the revised file, to open it up. Find and click once on Paste on the drop down Edit menu on the top toolbar. Your computer will ask you if you want to overwrite the current file that is on the floppy disc with the newly revised file, click Yes to paste in the revised version.

Earlier in the book we went over how to copy or move files into different folders using Windows Explorer. You can also copy or move files into different folders using the method we just went over. The following directions are for future reference if you want to copy or move files in this way.

-Highlight the document/ file that you want to copy or move by clicking once on it.

-Click once on the Edit button on the top toolbar. If you want to copy the file, click once on Copy. If you want to move the file, click once on Cut.

-Then, click on the Up One Level folder to find the folder that you want to copy or move the document/ file to. Double click on the folder to open it up.

-Click once on the Edit button on the top toolbar. Click once on the Paste button. Your file has now been pasted into this new folder.

*   *   *   *   *   *

Hopefully the projects that we have done so far have helped you to see all of the possibilities available to you with the programs that came installed with your computer. I now make my own designer envelopes and my flyers are colorful and eye catching. I also like to be on the look out for new and interesting fonts whenever I'm on the Internet. You can never have too many fonts! If you're interested in finding new fonts, also, just do your searching on the Internet the same way you search for clip art, etc. There are many free font websites to browse through.

7

Internet Basics

When I started surfing on the Internet, I was lost. It took me awhile to understand how to surf and when to surf. I found that there were times during the day when it was very difficult to get online and then to stay online. Now, if I want to really do some searching I get on the Internet early in the morning.

Some websites load very quickly because they don't have a lot of graphics. Others seem to take forever depending on the time of day and the amount of graphics that are on the web page. What I've learned in my Internet travels is how to organize my surfing, so that I don't get frustrated and I'll tell you some of my tricks. I'll also pass along addresses for some special websites and email newsletters.

Your Favorites

I believe that Favorites is one of the most useful features available with Internet Explorer. This feature allows you to save a website address so that you can view it later or keep it on file if it is a website that you will be going to often. When you place a website address in your Favorites file, your computer places it on the main menu list unless you tell it to organize it in a different way. After surfing for awhile, I found that my Favorites menu list became very long and difficult to view. So, I started organizing it.

To see what is on your Favorites menu right now, click once on the Start button in the lower left-hand corner of your screen. Move your pointer up to Favorites and then across to the menu. If you haven't added anything to your Favorites menu, there won't be very many titles on the menu list. You'll probably see Channels, Links, Media, etc. Some of the titles will have a right pointing arrow next to them. This means that there is a menu list within that folder. To access it just move your pointer up to a title with a right pointing arrow and this menu will appear.

You can set up your own category folders in the Favorites menu, so that when you visit a website you can place it in a specific folder. For instance, when I started doing research for software graphics programs I set up a folder titled Graphics. Then, if I saw a website that had graphics information, I put it in this folder so that I could find it easily later. We're going to practice setting up a few folders now. You have to be in your Internet Explorer window to organize your folders, so double click on the Internet Explorer icon on your Desktop to get connected.

-Find and click once on the Favorites button on the top toolbar of the Microsoft Internet Explorer window. At the top of the menu that drops down, you will see Add to Favorites…and Organize Favorites…. Move your pointer down and click once on Organize Favorites…to open that window.

-Find and click once on the button titled Create Folder. You'll notice that a new folder has been added to your menu list. It will be titled New Folder. Notice that it is highlighted with a blinking bar at the end of it. You can clear this title and rename the folder by hitting the Delete key on your keyboard. Do that now.

-Now you'll see an empty box with a blinking bar. Type Special sites and then hit the Enter key on your keyboard. You've just set up and named a new folder for your Favorites list. Great! You can close this window now. Let's find a special site to put in this folder.

-Move your pointer up to the white box next to Address. Now, move your pointer to the end of the website address that is in this white box and click once. You'll notice that the website address is now highlighted with a blinking bar at the end of it.

-Find the four arrows on your keyboard that are below your Delete key. Hit the left pointing arrow once. This will remove the highlighting effect and change your pointer into a cursor.

-Next, move your cursor and position it right after http://www.. Make sure that it is after the period at the end of www. Click and hold your mouse button and then move your cursor to highlight the rest of the website address. Hit the Delete key on your keyboard once. This will remove everything except http://www.. You can click in the white box, now, and then type in the following address, bestfriends.org. Doing it this way saves you the trouble of always having to type http://www. first. Once you've typed in this address, hit the Enter key on your keyboard and Explorer will take you to this website.

-Now that you are at the Best Friends website, let's save it in Favorites in the Special Sites folder that you just set up. Click once on the Favorites button on the top toolbar and then move your pointer down and click once on Add to Favorites…to open up that window.

-First, do you want to make this web page available for offline viewing later? If you do, click in the white box before Make available offline to put a check in this box.

-Now, look down and find Create in:. In the large white box next to it you'll see the menu list for the folders in Favorites. Find the new folder you set up titled Special sites. You may need to scroll down to find it. When you find it, click once on it to highlight it. Notice how the folder icon next to it now looks opened up. This means that it's ready for you to put something in it.

-Find and click once on the OK button in the upper right-hand corner. You've just added this website to your Special sites folder. Click once on the Close button in the top right-hand corner to close this window.

-You can visit the Best Friends website now, whenever you want to, without having to type in the address. Just click on the Start button in the lower left-hand corner, move your pointer up to Favorites and then across to the menu. Move your pointer to Special Sites and then across to the small menu. At this point you will only have Best Friends. After you place your pointer over Best Friends, click once on it and Internet Explorer will take you to this website. As you add website addresses to this folder, the menu will get larger.

-Let's set up some more folders for you to use later. You don't need to be online while we are doing this, so find the icon in the lower right-hand corner on the bottom toolbar that looks like two connected computers. Remember that this is the icon that shows you that you are connected to the Internet. Right click if you are right-handed or left click if you are left-handed to bring up the small menu. Move your pointer up and click once on Disconnect.

-Find and click again on Favorites on the top toolbar. Move your pointer down and click once on Organize Favorites...to open up that window. One of the folders that I use the most is one I set up and titled Go see when I have time. Sometimes, I'm in a hurry when I'm on the Internet. If I see a website that looks interesting, but I don't have the time right then to view it, I put it in this folder. Then, when I have some time, I go to this folder and pick out several websites to visit. Let's set up a folder for you with this title.

-Find and click on the Create Folder button. Hit the Delete key on your keyboard to remove the title New Folder. Now type, Go see when I have time, and then hit the Enter key on your keyboard. Waa Laa, another new folder!

Remember this next part for future reference. Let's say that you've added some new website addresses to this new folder to view later. It's now later and you've gone to several of the websites and viewed them. One of the websites was great and you would like to keep it in Favorites but in a different folder. The other website was not something that interested you and you want to get rid of it. Here's what to do with these two website addresses.

-Find and click once on Favorites on the top toolbar. Now, click on Organize Favorites…to open up that window. Find the folder titled Go see when I have time and click once on it. All of the website addresses listed in that folder will now appear below it. Find the website address of the site that you liked and would like to keep and click on it once to highlight it. You've decided that it is a special site and would like to put it in the Special sites folder. Now that you have highlighted it, find and click on the button titled Move to Folder….

-A new window titled Browse for Folder will open up. Find the folder titled Special sites on the menu list and click on it once to highlight it. Now, find and click once on the OK button. The address of the website that you liked has now been moved to this folder. Click once on the Close button in the upper right-hand corner to close the Browse for Folder window.

-You'll now be back in the Organize Favorites window. Find and click once on the address of the website that didn't interest you to highlight it. Next to the Move to Folder button, you'll see the Delete button. Click once on the Delete button to delete the address that you aren't going to keep. Your computer will ask you if you really want to delete it. Click once on the Yes button.

-Occasionally, I find that the title of a website address is lengthy and hard to understand. You can rename any of the website addresses that you have in your Favorites menu if you want to. If this is something you want to do in the future, find and click once on the website title that you want to rename to highlight it. Then find and click once on the Rename button next to the Create Folder button. Hit the Delete key on your keyboard once to delete the current name. Now type your new name and then hit the Enter key on your keyboard.

Maybe you already have website addresses in your Favorites file. Would you like to organize them? Do some of them have a common theme? If you do have website addresses listed and you would like to organize them, you can take some time now to set up folders and then move the addresses to these folders. Here are the titles of some of the folders that I have set up in my Favorites menu, Ecards, Special sites, Graphics, Newsletters, Go see when I have time, Desktop themes, Wallpapers, Screensavers, etc. Take a moment and look at the menu that is in the folder titled Links. Earlier in the book, I gave you addresses for search sites that you could visit. This folder is a good place to keep these addresses for search sites.

You'll probably find that once you start surfing on the Internet, your Favorites menu list will get longer and longer. If you create folders and keep your menu list organized in this way, I guarantee you that your surfing experience will be very pleasant.

How To Use Those Buttons

We're going to do a quick review of some of the buttons that are on the middle toolbar of your Internet Explorer window. These buttons are Back, Forward, Stop, Refresh, Search, History, Home, and Mail. If you aren't familiar with them, take a moment to find these buttons on the middle toolbar.

Let's begin with the Back and Forward buttons. When you connect to the Internet and visit your first website, these two buttons will look dark and recessed on the toolbar and you won't be able to use them. As you begin surfing to different websites, the back arrow will light up and appear three-dimensional. You can now use this button if you want to revisit a website that you viewed earlier. If you want to return to the website that you were just at, you can click once on the back arrow itself to go to this website. If you want to return to a website that you visited awhile ago, click once on the down arrow next to the Back arrow. The small menu that comes down will list the websites that you have visited.

Move your pointer down and click once on the website that you want to return to. You can also keep clicking on the back arrow until you are back at the website that you want to view.

Once you use the Back button to view previously visited websites, the Forward button will light up and appear three-dimensional. You can now use this button, also. If you want to return to the website that you were just at when you clicked on the Back button, click once on the Forward arrow itself to go to this website. If you want to go forward further than this, click once on the down arrow next to the Forward arrow. Again you will see a small menu. Click once on the website that you want to go forward to again.

If a website seems to be taking a very long time to download, you can click on the Stop button once to stop the download from continuing. Occasionally when Explorer connects to a website, you just don't get a very good connection or it has trouble connecting with the server. By stopping the download, you can tell Explorer to try again by clicking once on the Refresh button. More often than not, you'll find that when you do this, the website will download much faster. If you go to a website and a web page appears that says This page cannot be displayed, try clicking the Refresh button once. Usually this will correct the problem and the website will download. If you've chosen a time of day when you know that the Internet isn't busy, you probably won't have this problem.

I've learned to not even try to get on the Internet between the hours of 12 p.m. and 5 p.m. These are peak times where I live. I find it very frustrating when I have to wait for a long time for a website to download. You'll know that you are on the Internet during a peak time if you experience any of the following; very slow downloads on websites, suddenly and frequently being disconnected from the Internet, a busy signal when you try to connect, your computer telling you that it was not able to establish a connection or that there is a problem with your modem and you know that your modem is fine. Try to figure out when the peak times occur in your area and then do yourself a favor and don't surf during that time.

The next button on the middle toolbar is the Home button. If you click on the Internet Explorer shortcut icon on your desktop to access the Internet, the page that always shows up first is your home page. When you click on the Home button on your toolbar, you'll automatically go to this website, also. Your computer was probably sent with a specified website address already in place as your home page. You can change this and set up any website that you want as your home page. You can also access the Internet to begin with by clicking on a website address in your Favorites file. If you always use the Explorer shortcut, though, to get connected, it's nice to have one of your favorite websites as your home page. You can also change this feature whenever you want to and rotate your favorite websites if you'd like.

-To input the website that you would like to have as your home page, find and click once on the Tools button on the top toolbar. Move your pointer down and click once on Internet Options...to open up this window.

-Under the General tab, you'll see Home page. Next to Address: will be a white box with your current home page website address. If this website address is highlighted, and you would like to change it, click once at the end of the address in the white box to remove the highlighting effect. Move your cursor right behind www., click your mouse button and hold it while you move your cursor to highlight the rest of the address. Hit the Delete key on your keyboard once to delete the remainder of the address. I find this is the easiest way to change a website address, then I don't have to type in the http://, etc.

-Now, type in the rest of the website address that you would like set as your home page. Then find and click once on the Apply button in the lower right-hand corner of the window. Click once on the Close button to exit this window. If you chose to change the website address, your new home page is now set and you can change it again whenever you'd like.

If you're surfing and want to do a quick search about something, you don't have to surf to one of the search websites to do this. Find and click once on the Search button on your middle toolbar. A small window will be inserted next to and to the left of the window for the website that you are visiting. Just type in what you are searching for and then click the search button. A list of websites will be provided for you. Move your pointer to and double click on the website that you want to visit. If you want to visit other websites on this list, you'll need to leave this small window open. When you are done with this window, find and click on the small x in the upper right-hand corner of this small window to close it.

If you want to do a more refined search, you can go to one of the search sites that I listed before, i.e. msn.com, yahoo.com, metacrawler.com, and snap.com. To do a general search just type in what you looking for in the Search box on the main page of their website. Keep the wording simple. For example, if you are looking for websites that have teddy bears, type in teddy bears. To narrow your search down and make it more specific, look through the categories that are listed somewhere below the search box. Then, look to see if you can narrow it down even more by reading the subtitles below the category. When you've found a category or subtitle that is close to what you are looking for, click once on it. Read through what is listed on the new web page that opens up. If you can narrow your search down even more by clicking on any of the categories, do so. Or look for a search box where you can type in what you are looking for and then search for it just in that category.

Next, find the History button. The History file is a list of all the websites that you have visited in the past. This feature is very useful if you've visited a website and didn't put it in your Favorites folders and would like to see it again.

-To see how far back your History file goes, click once on the Tools button on the top toolbar. When the menu pops down, move your pointer down to Internet Options…and click once on it to open up this window.

-Under the General tab and towards the bottom of this window you'll see History. Under the title History, you'll see Days to keep pages in history:. There will be a small white box next to this with an up and down arrow. What number is in the white box? How many days back would you like your computer to store web pages for you? Since I surf the Internet quite a bit, this file would be very large if I had my computer store pages for me for a long time. So, I have mine set at 5 days. Decide how many days you would like your computer to keep pages for you and set the number in this box. Find and click once on the Apply button at the bottom of the window and then close this window.

Now, find and click once on the History button on the middle toolbar. Another window will be inserted next to the window for the website that you are visiting, with a list of websites that you've visited. If you click once on a website on this list, it will show you all the web pages that you visited at that particular website. You might have to do some searching, if it was a website that you visited a few days ago. To go to a website on this list, just double click on it.

If you click on the down arrow next to View that is under the title History, you can decide how you would like the list to be organized. I find that it is easier to view when it is organized by date. When you are done viewing the History list, click the small x in the upper right-hand corner to close this window.

The button next to History is the Mail button. Click the down arrow next to Mail to view the small menu. You'll see Read Mail…, New Message…, Send a Link…, and Send a Page…. If you want to read new messages that you may have received in your email program while you've been surfing the Internet, click on Read Mail. If you want to send a message, click New Message. What if you find a website that is so absolutely fabulous that you want to tell all of your friends about it or you find one that has really important information that would benefit a friend of yours? You can send the link or website address to them via email by clicking on Send a Link. You can also let them know about the website by clicking on Send a Page. I prefer sending a link, though, because I can type a short message to them if I want to.

There is another way to send a link or page by email to friends. Find and click once on File on the top toolbar. Move your pointer down to Send. Move your mouse over to the small menu that opens up and you'll see Page by Email…, Link by Email…, and Shortcut to Desktop. Click once on Link by Email. This will open up a new message in your email program with the link inserted. Some websites have this option of sending a link by email listed on their website. You can click on the button they have made available if you would like. However, the option is always available by accessing the File menu or the Mail button in Internet Explorer.

Interesting Places To Visit

As I stated earlier in the book, an alternative to doing searches at search sites is to check out your specific interest at the RingSurf website at ringsurf.com. Just type in the topic that you are searching for in the search box, and a list of webrings will be compiled. When you find a webring that sounds interesting to you, you can either start surfing the websites themselves or you can see them listed with descriptions of their sites.

Two of my favorite webrings are Ladies of the Heart at ladies-of-the-heart.com and Random Acts of Kindness at theraokgroup.com. Ladies of the Heart is a very large group of woman who are doing their best to create a loving place on the Internet. Random Acts of Kindness is a large group of women and men spreading peace, love, and kindness over the Internet and making a difference one person at a time. Both of these webrings are comprised of a variety of websites set up by people who are committed to making a positive difference in the world. Both of these webrings also have newsletters that are sent out to members. You can send in prayer requests or information that you would like to share with the group and have it included in these newsletters. If you'd like to know more about being a part of these two wonderful Internet organizations, visit the websites listed above. There are many great websites with a common theme listed at RingSurf. Take some time and peruse the categories listed and have fun surfing the Internet in a different way.

If you think you would like to begin receiving email newsletters, there are many interesting ones out there. Listed below are some that I have compiled to get you started, along with their website addresses so that you can learn more about them.

These are inspirational websites/newsletters written and sent out via email to uplift, inspire, and help you with the process of living in today's world. They are: Your Life Support System at LifeSupportSystem.com, Winning Without Intimidation at burg.com, Chicken Soup for the Soul at chickensoup.com, Angel Scribe at angelscribe.com, Heroic Stories at HeroicStories.com, Starfish at OhAngel.com/ Starfish, Heartwarmers at heartwarmers.com, and Two Scoops at twoscoops.com.

If you like a variety of beautiful photographs and interesting quotes, you're in luck. Daily Inbox is a newsletter that combines the two to provide you with an interesting and unusual newsletter. You can find them at DailyInbox.com. Arcamax always has interesting news and lots of free offers to pass on to you. You can find them at arcamax.com. Are you interested in unusual and unknown facts? If you are, the Did You Know newsletter is a great one to receive. Dazzle your friends with these unknown and sometimes bizarre facts. You can find information about this newsletter at didyouknow.com.

Would you like to learn more about the latest advances for computers? Lockergnome is a great newsletter to get you started. Chris Pirillo, the man who writes the newsletter, presents the computer information in a wonderfully witty and fun way. Often, I don't understand the more technical information that he provides, but I always find some tidbit that helps me along my computer path. Become a gnomie by visiting his website and signing up at lockergnome.com.

Have you ever received any of those strange emails that have information about some bizarre happening? For instance, I once received a forwarded email from a friend that claimed that Yahoo was selling stock at their China website. It gave a website address and encouraged you to get in on the ground floor. It was, of course, a huge hoax or what they call an urban legend. If you get any of these emails and want to check them out to see if they are true or not before sending them on to your friends, you can visit the Urban Legends References Pages information website at snopes.com. They also have a newsletter that you can sign up for. Be prepared when those weird emails show up in your mailbox with weird claims.

Do you like to give to the world but often don't have the time or finances to accomplish this goal? Check out the websites that I will be listing below to learn how to click and give! Even if you don't have the finances or time, you can quickly surf to one of these sites and donate just by clicking on the donate button. These organizations have sponsors lined up who will donate a certain amount of money for every click through donation that visitors make to the site. You can only click through once a day, though. I have these websites set up in my Special Sites folder in Favorites. I can quickly visit them everyday and donate. It's a wonderful idea, isn't it? Someone was really using their noggin when they started this new trend on the Internet. Take a few moments and visit these websites, you'll be glad you did. The Hunger Site at the-hungersite.com, Charity Frogs at charityfrog.org, Free Donation at free-donation.com, and The Rainforest Site at therainforestsite.com.

Two of my favorite websites are Best Friends Animal Sanctuary at bestfriends.org and Silent Unity at unityworldhq.org. Silent Unity is a prayer website. They have a group of people who are continually praying and you can submit your prayer request at any time through the website and have them pray for you. They say that there is great power in group prayer. I'm a believer, because I've seen it work. I think these people are earth angels. They are devoted to serving the world and helping individuals to find peace in their lives. They are located in Unity Village, MO.

Best Friends is the nation's largest no kill sanctuary for companion animals. They provide shelter, care, and love for abused and abandoned cats, dogs, and other animals. The animals come from all over the country and there are never fewer than 1,800 there on any given day. Animals are given the special care that they require and most of them are then ready to be adopted to good homes. There are some animals that come into the sanctuary, though, who are old, or sick, or who have suffered extreme trauma. These animals are guaranteed a loving home for life at the sanctuary, if they cannot be adopted. Best Friends mission is to help bring about a time when there are no more homeless pets and when every companion animal that is ever born can be guaranteed a good home with a loving family. They also want to bring an end, once and for all, to the killing of homeless animals. Best Friends is located in Angel Canyon outside of Kanab, UT. I think that it is more than just a coincidence that this amazing place is located in Angel Canyon. The people who live and work there are earth angels, also. I have had the privilege of spending time there, helping with the animals, and seeing what these people do. The time that I spent there is one of my most treasured memories. Please take some time and check out their website.

How About Your Own Website?

Have you ever thought about doing your own website? Do you have a cause that you feel strongly about or artwork that you would like to share with the world? Would you like to have a place where you can post photos and information about your family so that your friends can see them? Maybe you just want to do something silly and fun and creative with some ideas that you have. You can create a website about anything.

When I first started my Internet travels, the thought of having my own website never occurred to me. I though that, in order to design a website, you had to know HTML coding and how to work with graphics. I also thought websites were set up just for businesses and to supply people with information. I was under the impression that not only did they cost money to have, but that they cost a lot of money to set up, if you wanted a web designer to do one for you.

A friend of mine had suggested to me that I try to do something with Sherwood on the Internet. I couldn't imagine what that would be. She commented that maybe I should start a chat room about him. I hadn't even been to a chat room. But, I had heard people mention that they spent time in chat rooms. So, I thought I would go check one out. Once I figured out how to get into one, I started chatting with others who were there. I quickly left that one because the topic turned suddenly rank and it was definitely not my cup of tea.

Then I got more specific about the topic I wanted to chat with people about. I found a great chat room and spent about an hour there. At one point, one of the people there invited all of us to view his website and gave the address. So, I quickly went to his website and was surprised. It consisted of photos of himself and his friends and information about what he was doing in his life at that point. I went back to the chat room and started questioning him about his website. He had done it himself and it was free. And…he didn't even know HTML. He also commented on how easy it was to do. I quickly asked him to tell me where I could find information about doing one myself. I realized that I had just found a way to get Sherwood on the Internet. I was going to do a website myself.

After reviewing some of the places on the Internet that provided free webspace for people so that they could do their own website, I decided on

Geocities at Yahoo. Then, I started reading. I knew that I had basic web authoring tools installed on my computer, but what I found at Geocities was that they had a pagebuilder wizard. I could use the wizard to set up a website with one of their set templates or I could start with a blank project and make it exactly the way I wanted right there. They had graphics and backgrounds and all the information I would need to design my new website. By using the pagebuilder, I wouldn't have to worry about uploading all the pages that I might have designed using the authoring tools that I had. If I wanted to use pictures or graphics of my own, all I would have to do was find them in my folders while I was doing the website at Geocities and insert them. It almost sounded too easy.

Since I decided to start with a blank project, it was more difficult than if I had chosen one of the template designs. It was worth it, though, because I was able to make the website look just that way I wanted. My idea for the website was for it to have a very simple design. I wanted to include some of the color images from my book and have information about Sherwood and where people could find signed and limited copies of the first edition. I also wanted to encourage people to follow their dreams. I had a few of the color images scanned at a local copier and then inserted those where I wanted them.

What I ended up with, was a simple four-page website that is easy to maintain. I was so pleased! And…it was relatively simple to do. I found, though, that some people had a tendency to look down their nose at me when they found out that I used a pagebuilding wizard. It didn't bother me, though, because I had a great time creating the website and it was exactly what I wanted. I didn't need to know HTML and neither do you. Of course, if it is something that you would like to learn, then you should take the time and learn it. But, if you'd like to do a simple and fun website, without having to learn HTML, take some time and check out the website addresses that I will be providing below. These are some of the places that I have compiled for you that provide free webspace and web authoring wizards for people who want to set up their own websites.

With what you have learned in my book, you should be able to very easily understand how the different wizards are set up. Keep in mind, if you choose to use a wizard to create your website, that you will need to be on the Internet while you are designing it. Be sure to find a time to create it while online when it is not a peak time. Plan out beforehand how you want your website to look and write down the information that you want to type in. All of this will minimize the time you will need to spend online while you are creating. When you are done, tell all your friends about your new website. You can also submit your url, or website address, to many different search engines for inclusion in their database. If you want to increase the traffic to your new website even more, you can join one or several of the webrings at RingSurf that have websites similar to yours.

Here are the addresses of a few of the places where you can find free website information. Geocities at geocities.yahoo.com/ home, Homestead at homestead.com, Tripod at tripod.lycos.com, BeSeen at home. beseen.com, Fortune City at fortunecity.com, Xoom at xoom.com/ webspace, and MSN at communities.msn.com/personalhomepages.

If you do choose to set up your website at one of these places, be sure to carefully read their website guidelines. Certain restrictions do apply if you are planning on setting up a website where the webspace is provided for you free of charge.

*   *   *   *   *   *

Well, that's it for Internet Basics and we've come to the end of this book. Geez, I'm suddenly feeling at a loss for words! It's always hard to end a creative project and let it go. My goal was to help you enjoy your computer more and to help you to find ways to be more creative with it. Did I reach my goal? I hope so. Are you happy with the way your computer looks and sounds? Have you started searching for new images to add to your desktop? Did you enjoy learning how to create fun stuff with your Word program?

If you'd like to send me comments about the book, just go to Sherwoods' website at geocities.com/ sherwood_111 and you can email me from there. I'd love to hear about your learning experience and I hope that it was a pleasurable one. I certainly had a pleasurable experience writing this book and ended up learning many new things myself! Keep learning, keep growing, and don't be afraid of falling down now and then. It happens to us all!

**So long for now and
may your life be blessed
with many good things.**

Appendix

Symbols and Their Shortcut Keys

Monotype Sorts

	y ▌	x ▏
	u ◆	c ✻
` ✸	i ✳	v ❖
1 ☞	o ❑	b ☀
2 ☛	p ❐	n ■
3 ✓	[✳	m ○
4 ✔	] ✺	, ✌
5 ✕	\ ✲	. ✎
6 ✖	a ✿	/ ✏
7 ✗	s ▲	+shift key
8 ✘	d ❄	~ 99
9 ✚	f ❆	! ✂
0 ✐	g ✳	@ ✣
- ✑	h ✷	# ✄
= †	j ❉	$ ✄
q ❑	k ❋	% ☎
w ☽	l ●	^ ✤
e ✹	; ✜	& ✐
r ❐	' ⊗	* ☛
t ▼	z █	(✈

143

) ⊠	M ★	a 🎿
_ ❀	< ✚	s 🏄
+ ☞	> ⚐	d 🤾
Q ✳	? ✝	f 🏇
W ✳		g 🚣
E ✛		h 🏋
R ✺		j 🐬
T ✶	**Monotype Sorts 2**	k 🤸
Y ✹		l 🤼
U ✷	` □	' ⓘ
I ☆	1 ◆	z 🏍
O ✩	2 ◆	x 🐎
P ☆	3 ◆	c 🤺
{ •	4 ◆	v 🚣
} "	5 ◆	b 🏃
| '	6 ◆	n 🤸
A ✡	7 ◆	m 🚣
S ✳	8 ◆	, 🎾
D ♣	9 ◆	. ⛵
F ◆	0 ◆	/ 🎿
G ◇	- 👤	+shift key
H ★	q ✈	! ⚽
J ✪	w 🚌	@ ♻
K ☆	e 🚃	# 🐎
L ✬	r 🚢	$ ⛸
: ✚	t 🚲	% ⛸
" ✂	y 🚴	& 🛷
Z ✳	u 🚗	* 🏀
X ✳	i 🚶	(⚾
C ♣	o 🛶	) 🏈
V ✳	p ⛵	+ 🏀
B ✛	[✈	
	\ 🚁	

Webdings

Q		g
W		h
E	`	j
R	1	k
T	2	l
Y	3	;
U	4	'
I	5	z
O	6	x
P	7	c
A	8	v
S	9	b
D	0	n
F	-	m
G	=	,
H	q	.
J	w	/
K	e	+shift key
L	r	~
"	t	!
Z	y	@
X	u	#
C	i	$
V	o	%
B	p	^
N	[	&
M	]	*
>	\	(
	a	_
	s	+
	d	Q
	f	W

Wingdings

Key	Key	Key
E	`	h
R	1	j
T	2	k
Y	3	l
U	4	;
I	5	'
O	6	z
P	7	x
{	8	c
}	9	v
|	0	b
A	-	n
S	=	m
D	q	,
F	w	.
G	e	/
H	r	+shift key
J	t	~
K	y	!
L	u	@
:	i	#
"	o	$
Z	p	%
X	[	^
C	]	&
V	\	*
B	a	(
N	s	)
M	d	_
<	f	+
>	g	Q
?		W
		E

Wingdings 2

Key		Key		Key	
R	✿	`	!	g	✺
T	❄	1	⬚	h	✺
Y	✡	2	⬚	j	①
U	✝	3	🗑	k	②
I	✋	4	⬚	l	③
O	☞	5	⬚	;	🛍
P	☜	6	🖥	'	☎
{	✿	7	📠	z	❻
}	"	8	⊙	x	❹
|	✾	9	⬛	c	∞
A	✌	0	⬚	v	❷
S	◆	-	▤	b	∞
D	✍	=	☟	n	⑤
F	☞	q	⑧	m	④
G	☝	w	❸	,	▤
H	☝	e	∾	.	▤
J	☺	r	⑨	/	⬚
K	☹	t	❿		
L	☹	y	❺	+shift key	
:	💻	u	❶	~	❿
"	✂	i	⓪	!	✏
Z	☾	o	⑥	@	☞
X	✠	p	⑦	#	✐
C	☝	[	&	$	✑
V	✝	]	!	%	✂
B	🤞	\	&	^	!
N	☠	a	∞	&	✂
M	💣	s	❿	*	⬚
<	💾	d	∞	(	☎
>	☣	f	∾	)	▤
?	✍			+	☟
				Q	⊠
				W	⊘

Wingdings 3

Key	Symbol	Key	Symbol	Key	Symbol
E	☛	`	⇦	g	→
R	☑	1	↔	h	↑
T	☒	2	↕	j	↖
Y	ℰ	3	⇠	k	↗
U	⊗	4	⇢	l	↙
I	⬮	5	↑	;	↪
O	✗	6	↓	'	←
P	✓	7	↯	z	▼
{	➐	8	↵	x	◣
}	➒	9	↳	c	⇨
|	➑	0	↨	v	◁
A	☛	-	↖	b	⇦
S	☒	=	↥	n	↔
D	☛	q	▼	m	↘
F	✐	w	▷	,	↧
G	✑	e	⇨	.	↘
H	✒	r	△	/	↨
J	✋	t	◀	+shift key	
K	✌	y	◤	~	▲
L	☟	u	▶	!	←
:	✍	i	↓	@	↵
"	✏	o	↕	#	↑
Z	&	p	▲	$	↓
X	⊘	[	⇨	%	↖
C	☞	]	⇨	^	⇦
V	⊗	\	⇦	&	↗
B	☜	a	⇨	*	⇥
N	✋	s	▽	(	↘
M	☝	d	⇦	)	⇤
<	☝	f	←	_	⇨
>	☜			+	↥
?	☞			Q	▼

W ↲
E ↕
R ↻
T ∧
Y ⇧
U ↰
I ⇉
O ↩
P ↺
{ ◣
} ▶
| ⇦
A ↳
S ⤨
D ⇄
F ⇶
G ⇲
H ⇇
J ⇈
K ⇊
L ∩
: ↵
" ↑
Z ⇦
X ⇧
C ⇲
V ↲
B ↴
N ↪

M ↺
< ↧

> ⌐
? ⌐

Silly Symbol Email Attachment

*   *   *   *   *   *

[hand] [smiley] [heart],

When you and Sandi [phone] 'd tonight about your [monitor], I meant to tell you not to feel [frown]. Your [monitor] won't [bomb]. Just remember the [key] is [yin-yang]. [lightning] won't strike your [house] or [monitor] if you make a mistake. Just whistle a happy [notes] [notes] and everything will be all right. When you go on your walks in the morning, remember to wear your [sunglasses], that NM [sun] can be really bright. When you play Solitaire or Freecell, remember to alternate the [spade] [club] suits, with the [heart] [diamond] suits. And check your e-[mailbox] often for e-[envelope].

I'm looking forward to [mail] my new [book] on my [monitor]. Maybe I'll write several [books], since it will cost a lot less [moneybag] to publish. With the new [monitor] technology, anything is possible. I've been spending so much time sitting, I think I need to [bicycle] or [dumbbell] or [rowing] to tone up my muscles. By the way, your [flower] [flower] garden looks great.

I'm [eye] ing forward to [plate] ing with you and [running] ing with you and [note] ing to you all on [sun] day. We'll probably have coffee instead of [cocktail] 's. And there will probably be many different [female] and [male] at the restaurant.

My [monitor] has been such a [gift] in my life and I [heart] playing on it. Can you tell? I'd better go, so I can get ready for [bed]. [wave] 's to you both. I'll see you at [clock] on [sun] day.

X X X 's and [lips] [lips] 's,

[dove] and [heart],
Cindy

*   *   *   *   *   *

Fantastic Fonts
Fonts used in Windows 98-2nd Edition

Abadi Condensed – **Abadi Extra Bold** – Abadi Light – Algerian – american – Andy – Arial – **Arial Black** – Arial Narrow – 1 - Arial Rounded MT Bold — 1 - AUGSBURGER - Baskerville - Bauhaus - BEESKNEES - Bernard- Blackadder - Book Antiqua – Bookman– Bradley Hand – Braggadocio ▪ Britannic - Broadway – Brush Script – Calisto – CASTELLAR – Century Gothic – Chiller - Comic Sans- Cooper Black – COPPERPLATE BOLD — COPPERPLATE LIGHT — Courier New – Curlz – DESDEMONA - EddA – Edwardian - Elephant – Enviro - Eurostile – FELIX – Forte – Franklin – Freestyle - French - Garamond – Georgia – Gigi – Goudy Old - GOUDY STOUT – Gradl – Harlow – Harrington – Impact – Imprint – Informal Roman – Jokerman – Juice - Kino – Kristen – Kunstler Lucida Calligraphy - Lucida Console – Lucida Handwriting - Lucida Sans - Lucida Sans Unicode - Maiandra – MATISSE - Matura – Mercurius – Mistral - Modern – Monotype – News – OCR A - OCRB – Old English – Onyx – Palace – Papyrus – Parade – Pepita – Perpetua – PERPETUA TITLING – Placard – Playbill - Poor Richard – Pristina – Rage - Ransom - Rockwell - Rockwell Extra Bold - Runic –Script – Snap - STENCIL - STOP – Tahoma – Tempus – Times New Roman – Tw Cen – TW Cen condensed – Verdana – Verdana Ref – Viner – Vivaldi - Vladimir – Westminster – Wide Latin

About the Author

Cindy Robison is a former computer illiterate. She bought her first computer at the age of 41 and now considers herself a passionate computer convert. In her new book, I Love My 'Puter, she shows computer beginners, through simple instructions and fun projects, how to enjoy their new computers.